Two Lives to a Destiny

Patrick Kimmell

ISBN: 978-1-952263-93-4

Dedication

This story is dedicated to all who have a vivid imagination
for reading books based on fiction.

So vivid, that they may become a reality!

Even while being based in the 18th century.

Acknowledgment

I cannot express enough gratitude to the people who have been patient enough with me in realizing this first novel. The experience was indeed exhilarating as well as exhaustingly pleasant, but quite valuable in the end. Much appreciation to all of you!

My deepest gratitude goes to my caring and loving wife, Fatima. The completion of this story would have never been if I hadn't met her. As fate would have it, I was offered a unique ingredient that enabled me to steer this story to its destination. It was its destiny.

Finally, to all those who have encouraged me to stay on this path, for simply having faith that I could actually be this person, an author. I hope you all enjoy this story as much as I enjoyed your encouragement. Thank you! My heartfelt gratitude to you all!

About the Author

Patrick Kimmell is the optimist. A smiley person with a fantastic imagination for creation. His distracted mind will always find comfort in the world of fiction and fantasies. "Where else would you ever want to live the ultimate dream! Just listen, and your mind will take you there … It knows the way." His words!

Is Patrick an author? This book might make you think he is, or it might even make you think that he might become one, but he has landed here purely by being a leisure music composer – a mind filled with notes.

Is Patrick recognized as a music composer? Of course not, he is too shy to be in the spotlight, but that might have to change. Not that you'd notice his timidity if you met him, but he is indeed gifted with the art of music composition.

Since most of his music tells a story, one day, he decided to write a story and create music from its scenery. This is how *Two Lives to a Destiny* came to life.

Preface

This is a tale of love and adventure that will take you to an array of places as it courses through a path, we all call destiny. It's an exciting journey of lovers who meet for the first time, fall in love unexpectedly, unprepared, and unaware of the quests that lie ahead just so that they can meet – only another time. But is this really their destiny? Set in the early seventeen hundred, this is the story of two souls who challenge and overcome societal obstacles erected by their different origins, cultures, and traditions.

But regardless of what is and what is not – there is harmony, friendship, commitment, and true love that feed the sublime stream of dreams and push anyone beyond the limits in ways they could have only imagined. Two people living separate lives will be tested through a sensational maze of encounters in an attempt to live the unique possibility of sharing a common goal – *"Love."*

Let the journey begin ...

Contents

Page Left Blank Intentionally

Chapter 1
The Dark Night

Awakened during the night, a crow drifts through the moonlit skies in search of an early prey. It's quiet – way too quiet – and perhaps not an ideal time to go out looking for sustenance, but the crow's hunger gets the best of it.

It flies around – a lone bird in the skies. It was going to be a good day for it. Soaring above rooftops in the dark, it tries to keep a sharp eye out for any movement on the brick roads below, but the mist is too thick for its eyes. It descends lower, piercing through the white mist that obstructs its view.

Flying down to the grounds penetrating the mist, a thick humid film waxes its glossy black plumage as it perches itself on a street lantern, unlit because the candle inside has faded. The streets are motionless – perfect because it means little or no distractions as it proceeds with its intended task. The crow takes off from the lantern to scout the surrounding area for food, but as it settles upon a tilted hay wagon to feed on the leftover grain, something else catches its eye.

A sneaky rodent is crawling out of the sidewalk sewer. The hungry crow swiftly charges towards its prey to make sure it does not run back into its dingy hideout. Just as the crow engages its attack towards the little rodent, it is distracted by the sound of a coachman's whip.

Seconds later, a pair of magnificent black Clydesdale horses come out of nowhere right in front of the crow. They are pulling a luxurious black coach with lustrous golden trims bringing the smallest glimpse of light in the night so dark.

Startled, the crow lets out a loud cry ranting the silent air and hastily changes course upwards to avoid a collision with either the horse or the coach. It adeptly escapes the close call and finds itself a rooftop to perch on. Once again, it is above the thick mist, now beginning to disappear ever so slowly as the time for the dawn draws near.

From its comfortable position on the rooftop, the crow watches the coach silently drive away into the night.

With the coach gone, the crow coasts back down to the tilted hay wagon and eagerly looks around for its prey. The calm of the fading night has restored now, but everything is still dark. Undefined shadows rule the night, but the crow is not bothered by them. It is more interested in the scent of fresh blood that he's just picked up in the air. The scent leads the crow down the brick road once again. This time it finds the little rodent lying lifelessly just a few feet away from the sidewalk where the coach had trampled it. The crow looks down at the rodent's redundant corpse, picks it up with its big black beak, and carries it beside the haystack.

It can finally enjoy a meal now – or maybe not. Just as it prepares to sink its beak into the little rodent, a man runs out into the street where the coach had disappeared just moments before.

The man seems terrified. It is as if he has just seen a ghost. The dark night is not making it any better for him as he desperately sprints forward, without any sense of direction. He is out of breath. He comes to a halt and looks around in confusion. There is despair all over his face.

He is trembling. It couldn't have been because of the cold, though. The night, although slightly chilly, was still comfortably warm.

There is obviously something worrying him. The man glimpses at the haystack in the wagon the crow had previously been perched on. He then looks back to where he has come from, turns around, and stares at the hay wagon again – as if contemplating something. His expression settles as he has just made up his mind about something that had been bothering him. The man then limps towards the haystack laden wagon, scaring the crow away who is silently witnessing the entire scene unfurl from the sidewalk, away from his meal.

The man reaches the wagon and quickly covers himself with the hay, erasing all existence of his presence. He is hiding from someone or something. The man is breathing heavily, trying desperately to bring his respiration under control. From a distance, the crow can see the man struggling, but there is something else in sight of the crow that the man is oblivious to.

There is another man. He comes out of the same street as the man hiding in the hay, but unlike the limping man, this one is not perturbed. Rather, he seems quite composed as he moves in the dark with a glistening sword in one hand and a lantern in the other. The swordsman lifts the lantern high up in the air above him, allowing the light to illuminate the surroundings, and then cries out loud.

"You won't be able to hide forever, heretic!"

His voice thunders through the dead silence that the crow had gotten accustomed to in this unfortunate night. It voices out its frustration with a broken cry, but the humans in the town are nonchalant to it. A hungry bird is perhaps the last thing on their list of priorities, and rightly so. The crow does not know what to expect next, but it can sense the tension building up between the men.

It wants to help the heretic, and the only way it knows how it is to cry out warnings for him. So, the crow cawed. It can see the swordsman walk around the area, searching for the heretic; his sword held low enough to allow its sharp steel blade to screech every time it came in contact with the brick road. The man in the haystack sits there motionless, his eyes closed out of fear. He listens to the cawing crow, wondering what it's doing awake at this hour.

His heart is pounding madly against his chest as if it'll jump right out of his body the first chance it gets. He can hear the screeching sword drawing near – just like his impending doom. The heretic is petrified. He knows his end is near. As beads of perspiration glide down the side of his face, the heretic finds his mind chanting a continuous silent prayer. He wants to live. He squeezes his eyes shut tightly – the prayer is a constant cadence that his mind keeps playing repeatedly.

"Please, Lord, please ... save me."

Suddenly, the screeching stops. He knows the swordsman is standing close by, but he is unaware that the vile man is stationed right next to the haystack, preparing to stab it. A torrent of memories flashes through the heretic's mind. He tries to hold on to each one for as long as he can just to relive them one more time before he dies at the hands of the merciless swordsman. Something at the back of his mind keeps reminding him that there isn't much time left for him to do that.

The swordsman raises his sword, ready to stab the haystack. He isn't sure if the heretic is actually in there or not, but it is worth a try. After all, he has nothing to lose.

Just when he almost plunges the sword into the pile of hay, a voice calls out to him.

"He's over here; we should cut him off at the bridge."

The swordsman pauses midway, glaring blankly at the haystack. This hunt is testing his patience. He hadn't thought it would take him this long to end the sorry life of a heretic, but he had escaped before he could serve justice.

Angry, the swordsman lifts his weapon and sways away some hay off the wagon before sliding his blade back into his belted scabbard. He then runs off to join his fellow men back at the bridge. Concealed beneath the hay, the heretic waits a few minutes – each of which seems to be longer than eternity – before letting out a deep sigh of relief. He waits a couple of minutes more and finally crawls off the wagon.

He is out of danger – temporarily. He knows the swordsmen would come back looking for him when they do not find him at the bridge and that didn't give him much time to escape. If he really wanted to live, the heretic had to act quickly and make the most of this short window of opportunity he had been blessed with.

He stands up straight next to the wagon and begins sweeping off the hay straws stuck on his clothing. Knowing he does not have much time to spare, the heretic looks around. He spots a dark alley not too far from where he stands.

"That's it. That's my doorway out of this nightmare," he says, talking to himself. He promptly makes his way to his left.

"That was way too close. Thank you, Lord, for letting me live my life another day," he says, sniffing softly, still talking to himself, glancing skyward as he mentions the Lord. It is indeed something to be grateful for. The crow sees the last of this man as it flies away with its prey in its beak, finally feeling grateful for the food it has managed to acquire.

The heretic had never thought he was going to live past tonight. It had all begun when the heretic had stood up to the powerful lord who looted and plundered towns for both business and pleasure. Anyone who disagreed with him faced the same fate – death. It had been a short while, give or take six months that the heretic and his family had moved to this peculiar town.

Peculiar, because he had never seen people submit to a criminal monarchy the way the locals here did. They appalled him, yet he felt responsible for showing them the right path. Little did he know what he was getting into – being ruthlessly murdered at the hands of goons was never in the equation, or perhaps, the heretic hadn't surmised the gravity of this situation. He had refused to bow down. He had refused to submit. And then there was the lustrous black carriage waiting outside his home. They had decided to kill him. The heretic shuddered at the thought as he hastened towards the small dark alley. He felt a chill run down his spine, and even though it wasn't cold, he wrapped his arms around himself in an attempt to rub the chill away.

They did warn him, though. Before they actually showed up at his door, the heretic did remember receiving subtle threats, but he had never fathomed they were to be taken seriously. Now, he was regretting his decision. He should have just left town when the first warning had asked him to do so. He could have started a new life somewhere else. But his wife loved it here. His sweet wife – had it not been for her, he would have been dead by now. It all still seemed like a nightmare. They had been awakened in the dead of night by the fierce rapping on their front door. His wife had immediately leaped out of bed to check on their little daughter, who was peacefully dreaming in her cradle.

Meanwhile, the heretic had walked to the front door. The knock was thunderous. It had almost been as if the door would break open if he didn't open it in the minutes that followed. He had been able to hear the distant stomping of hooves – whoever it was, they had come with tired horses, or they were just restless. *"I know you're in there; come out right now, or I'll take this door apart,"* the fierce voice outside had roared through the door.

The heretic had the sense that there was something wrong. He had never had visitors this late, let alone ones who threatened to break in if not allowed inside. His instinct had screamed at him quite loudly against opening the door, but the heretic had unbolted it still.

The doorway had been blocked by a figure that towered well over him. The heretic, still squinting in the dark to make out who this unexpected visitor was, had been taken by surprise when the giant man grabbed him by his collar and pulled him out of the house. His feet got off the ground. He was elevated enough to see that the man was not alone. He had others waiting for him in the carriage. At that precise moment, the man dropped him to the ground. The heretic had faltered; his eyes set on the shadow on the ground that kept getting bigger with each heartbeat. He tried to warn his wife to stay inside, just as the huge man towering above him drew his gleaming sword out of its scabbard. *"You were warned! We told you to leave this town and go away. Must you not listen! You called this upon yourself,"* said the man.

"Who sent you?" the heretic hated the way his voice had trembled with fear. He was all but whimpering like a kitten that had just been rescued from a gushing river. Only this time, he wasn't being rescued.

"You're going to die. Right here, in front of your pathetic wife. We'll then drag you through the town to let the people know the outcome of going against the master," said the man.

He had raised his sword to take the final plunge at his target, but before he could launch the sword into the heretic, a splash of fiery, hot water bounced against his face taking him by surprise but more importantly blinding him for the moment.

"Run," his wife had said. *"Don't worry about the baby and me."*

The last he had seen of her was when she had hastened into the dark house, while he had managed to get up and make the run. If only he hadn't bumped his bad knee into the side of the carriage, he would have escaped before the men caught up to him. He was still limping, but at least he didn't have to run for his dear life at the moment.

He was thankful for this chance. He said a small prayer for his wife and daughter's safety while he was away from them. He had reached the opening to that alley – his doorway out of this terrible nightmare. He felt relieved and at peace.

He would soon be out of this mess. He was just a limp away from freedom. He quickly turned into the alley, not knowing what was waiting for him.

A shiny silver blade pierced through his back and brought him to a complete stop. Blood spattered in the street all around him. Gasping for air, the heretic stared at the big feather that was stuck in a mysterious hat above his attacker's head. The attacker had moved in front of him to look into his eyes as the light of life left them.

The heretic lowered his gaze and glanced at the aggressor's cold eyes – like daggers of steel – slowly fading into the darkness's shadows as he caved in to the pain.

The heretic knew who it was. Those eyes could not be mistaken for anyone else's.

"Praying too much tonight, are we?" the man in front of him added with a smirk.

The heretic swallowed audibly as he formed the words *"Garra ... del ... Dia,"* but before he could finish what he had wanted to say, the man with the feathered hat twisted the dagger clockwise and pushed the heretic off the blade. The heretic fell to the ground like a puppet without strings.

Looking upon the heretic with contempt, the aggressor pulled out a cloth. Embroidered with the monarchy's emblem. He used it to wipe his dagger.

The heretic lay lifeless on the ground in a pool of his own blood, which had already begun clotting. The man who had killed him stood silently, staring at his doing. The man smirked again, dropped the blood-stained cloth next to the dead heretic, and inserted the now clean dagger back into his cane. He then turned around and walked away into the shadows leaving the heretic to succumb to his wound.

Chapter 2
The Story Begins

That same morning, off the shores of Gibraltar, the sun rose at its brightest. A fresh but swift breeze accompanied the warmth of the sun, which indicated that this day would be perfect for sailing.

At the port of Gibraltar, a young captain named Patrick ordered his crew to load the cargo ship for their routine shipment to Tangier.

Tangier, a historical city in northern Morocco, was once conquered by the English for their advantage. Still, then it was deliberately destroyed by the British army following the crippling blockade imposed by the Sultan of Morocco. Tangier's city was a mess until the Sultan rebuilt it into a bustling port city where all the major trade of the country took place.

Patrick, a native to Gibraltar, was born to Catherine and her husband. Catherine was the widow of a highly ranked and decorated officer of the Spanish Navy, who had unfortunately died of yellow fever during the war of the

Grand Alliance. She had been pregnant with their son when this misfortune had happened. Thus, Patrick – now a handsome young man in his late twenties, was inevitably obliged to grow up without a father figure.

He had never seen his father, but Patrick had no regrets about that. It was a void he had made peace with because it had undoubtedly been fulfilled gracefully by his mother.

Catherine had always been an easygoing person. Even when adversity struck when she had been left alone to tend to her son's needs and education as a single mother, Catherine never lost her calm. She had always been a simple woman who had no greater expectations from life than the one she was given. Perhaps that was her most intriguing charm.

She had grown up in England. She was a nurse by profession. It had been her passion for helping others that had arguably led her into this noble profession.

Wars surged in countries everywhere around the world. She had known her services would soon be called upon elsewhere; she could just feel it. The inevitable happened sooner than she had expected. Her skills and services were required in Gibraltar at the English Royal Navy base. At first, she had been a little terrified about moving to a country she had never seen, but in her mind, she was convinced that fate had allowed her to serve where she was most valued.

What she did not know back then was that the same place would soon become the place she calls home. One night while she had been on duty, a peculiar event happened that changed her life as she knew it.

A Spaniard dressed in a British uniform came into her quarters with severe injuries. She had already noticed that this soldier was not one of the British soldiers, but regardless of what she knew, she took it upon herself to care for him. Fate has its sneaky ways in presenting itself and Catherine was entirely unaware at the time that she would fall in love with this man and, better still, bear his child.

They met secretly for several months after that fortunate night when Catherine had tended to his wounds, but once he had completely healed, he had to rejoin his fleet. On the day of his departure, he promised Catherine that he would come back for her as soon as the war ended. None of them knew that this was a promise that he would not be able to honor. He left never to return, and that was the last time Catherine saw him. Shortly after, Catherine gave birth to a healthy baby boy. She named him Patrick. Even in the absence of his father, Patrick had a wonderful childhood. As a new-born baby, he had never been cranky, and as he grew up, he took to the easygoing ways of his mother.

He was a sprightly teenager who continued exceeding all expectations as he transitioned into the fine young man he was today. His deep blue eyes on his ocean-tanned face looking out six feet above the ground with the wind flowing through his dark brown hair gave him the ultimate confidence any man could ever ask for. He seemed to have it all, and most would say that he did, but something was missing in his life, or should we say, someone.

Patrick did not have a lady love in his life, although many maidens would have given their lives to be with him. Patrick just had one mistress – his cargo ship – he was, without a doubt, committed to sailing. The only woman in his life was his mother, and he was a doting son to her, taking good care of her – the woman who had sacrificed a good part of her life to educate him the best she could.

"Patrick!"

Patrick turned around to seek the source of the voice upon hearing his name. He looked out towards the anchorage. Miguel was gesturing him to get off the ship. Without hesitation, Patrick walked down the ramp onto the dock and made his way towards Miguel.

Miguel was born in Spain to a low-income family that had moved to Gibraltar in search of work and better opportunities. Despite belonging to a destitute background, Miguel held values that were always realistic. Fate indeed has its way of turning things around, and Miguel became truly fortunate after his sister married a wealthy Dutch shipbuilder. This changed his life dramatically. The Dutchman was affluent but also generous to his wife's family.

He believed that everyone deserved an equal chance to succeed in life. The man knew Miguel had spent most of his life working on cargo ships and acquired lots of experience from mostly living on them, so he decided to open the door to Miguel's business world. He offered to finance twelve brand new Dutch cargo ships for him to run his own company. Miguel did not hesitate to accept the offer, and once the contract was drafted and signed, the Dutchman pulled a few strings within his political cult to make sure Miguel had an elite clientele to service. In a short period of time, Miguel had a fleet of cargo ships ready for business. His ships were permitted to sail anywhere he wanted as long as he kept himself out of mischief, which meant keeping the cargo legal. This was back in the eighteenth century, near the end of the era of the Golden Age of Piracy.

The Dutchman had made it clear that cargo delinquency would put an end to Miguel's career, which Miguel understood very well. He was much older than Patrick. He was also a seasoned sailor who observed and recognized the natural ship navigating skills Patrick had since a noticeably young age. They had worked on the same ship for several years. Miguel acknowledged this young man's talent, but there was also the fact that he always had a soft spot for Catherine.

Miguel's feelings for Catherine probably had a bit of influence upon his decision about Patrick's fate when he had promoted him as Captain on one of his ships. Although nothing ever became serious between Miguel and Catherine, there was one thing sure; they both got along quite well when they were together.

Patrick approached Miguel to realize that his boss had a concerned look on his face, an expression he didn't see very often unless something was awfully wrong. Miguel turned his back to Patrick and started walking on the walkway towards his office, gesturing Patrick with a wave of his hand to follow him. The walkways, built with stone, connected the port to a huge enclosed shipyard where Miguel's ships were serviced or repaired when damaged. Next to the shipyard, stood a colossal two-story industrial brick building, built to store all local and foreign trade goods.

All the lightweight goods like linen cloth, wool, and silk rolls were stored on the top floor, and the heavier items went to the main floor. There were two stables at the rear of the building, one to store animals before they were shipped and the other to take care of Miguel's horses and coach. Miguel's luxurious office was also on the main floor in the middle of the building, from where he could see all his ships arriving and departing with their cargos. Regardless of the time of the day, Miguel was always present when his ships were scheduled for arrival. On their way to the office, treading on the rugged path, Miguel informed Patrick that they needed to discuss a few issues. Patrick was tempted to ask what about, but he knew Miguel better than that. His boss preferred secrecy in business matters, and the only reason he confided in Patrick was that he trusted him with them. Miguel opened the creaky wooden door and invited Patrick inside, motioning him to sit down.

Miguel walked behind his freshly waxed cherry oak desk and poured Patrick and himself a glass of water. In a fairly cautious manner, he explained to Patrick that two things needed to be addressed urgently.

He relaxed into his luxurious Louis XV designer chair and reached into his pocket to pull out an old folded piece of cloth. He wiped the sweat off his light-bearded face and stretched his arm out, still holding onto the cloth. With his arm fully extended, he looked at the cloth and then glanced into Patrick's eyes, dropped the cloth while holding a corner, and waving it at him, *"Sails."*

Patrick quietly observed his boss' peculiar ways and sat listening to him attentively. He knew what his boss was hinting at. This discussion was inevitable. During the last year, his ship had a questionable amount of sails repairs, and this was surely not going to go unseen – especially when the cost had been exceptionally high for each repair.

"Are we finally getting new ones?" The suggestion made Patrick uncomfortable, and he fidgeted in his seat. In an attempt to evade the truth, Patrick had replied in a surprised tone pretending to look around at the majestic décor in Miguel's office.

His response made Miguel laugh while thinking that the money he had spent in the last year on repairing old sails was enough to buy new sails for two of his ships. Miguel then replied, nodding his head, *"Knots has to go, son."*

Patrick almost choked on the water upon hearing Miguel's suggestion and affirmed himself, saying, *"That cannot and will not be arranged."*

Knots was one of Patrick's most loyal shipmates. The suggestion obviously did not sit well with him, even though he knew that Knots had trouble tying a knot that could withstand high winds, and ironically, this is how he had gotten his unconventional nickname.

Knots had been born and raised in an orphanage in Portugal. His life had always been a series of continuous rejections from the society he was a part of. Life had not been kind to him either, especially when it came to work. He was a reedy little man, clumsy most of the time, easily intimidated by others, and extremely shy around people. Knots' main issue was that he had little self-confidence, but what he lacked there, he made up for it with his big loving heart and eagerness to help anyone in any way he could. However, even though his intentions were always pure, he usually ended up getting himself into trouble. Eventually, fate opened up a path for him that compensated him for his kindness and respect towards humanity.

Once, he had managed to get a crowd in a Gibraltar marketplace quite angry. Someone in the group had pushed him so hard, that he fell to the ground. As soon as he hit the concrete, Knots was trampled by a coach horse that was passing by.

Catherine happened to be in the market that same day. She witnessed the cruelty that led to his accident. She just couldn't help herself from tending to the injured young man before her. She quickly approached him and helped him up, off the ground, wiping the dirt off his clothes. She offered him to come home with her so she could tend to his wounds. As she helped him get up, Catherine felt the goodness in the little man's heart. She was not afraid to help him. Knots, on the other hand, was baffled by what had shaken him the most – being trampled by a horse or offered help by a sweet lady. It was the first time someone had actually offered to help Knots, and he gladly accepted Catherine's generous offer and followed her home. After she had patched up his wounds, Catherine prepared a meal for Knots. As he sat eating quietly, she patiently tried to muster up a conversation with him, but Knots was mostly unresponsive in the presence of so much food.

This went on until Catherine mentioned the word *"work."* She was a wise woman who quickly understood that Knots was looking for a job and would do anything for work. He got up in the middle of the conversation to show her that he could sweep and wash floors, do dishes, and clean windows. He even pulled her outside to show her that he could chop wood too, regardless of his injury. His English language proficiency was nil.

This made Catherine laugh, but she had a better idea, and she didn't hesitate to share it with him. Knots was in a conundrum after Catherine apprised her idea to him, but he felt he was on a roll, and an opportunity was finally knocking at his door. So, once he finished his meal, they both headed out to the docks. At the docks, Patrick was recruiting shipmates for the new cargo ship Miguel had offered him. Catherine thought this could be a good place for Knots to work. As soon as they arrived at the port where Patrick was recruiting, Knots was clearly in awe of the new early edition of the Gotheborg cargo ship. He was amazed at the sight of the ship. He felt an urge to get a closer look at it. Giving in to it, he ran swiftly onto the ship, up the main mast to the crow's nest, and walked side to side on the topgallant mast. At that moment, he had already caught everyone's attention.

Everyone on the dock had their eyes locked on him. They seemed quite impressed, but at the same time feared that he might fall off the mast. Patrick was quick to recognize Knots' agility. Keeping his eyes on the young man, he asked him to come down, slowly and carefully. Patrick's mind was made up, but no one became a shipmate without passing a physical exam, which was done on-site at the docks. When Knots came up to him, Patrick stretched out his hands to Knots' chin and forehead and opened his mouth to inspect his teeth, lowered his head to inspect his hair for ticks and fleas, turned him around a few times and then affirmed his decision in a loud, clear voice, *"Hired!"*

The crowd roared with laughter, and Knots became a permanent member of Patrick's crew. He was assigned two main tasks on the cargo ship. He was responsible for the bird's view in the crow's nest and securing the sails on the mainmast. Since then, Knots had been working for Patrick to the best of his abilities. However, his best was not good enough for Miguel's business. The expenses for repairing sails now and then were running high, and while Patrick was aware of it, he just wasn't ready to let go of Knots. The discussion on Knots' fate continued in Miguel's lavish office, and Patrick stood his ground, repeating his stance in different words, *"By far, this will ever be fate."*

Patrick knew he had to fight for Knots. It was the least he could do for the man's unwavering loyalty to him. Plus, Knots was part of his crew, and his crew was like a family to him. He stood up from his seat without losing sight of Miguel, placed both his hands on the table and challenged Miguel's suggestion, *"My crew has exquisitely outperformed every ship in your fleet throughout the year filling your pockets with coins; much more than needed to maintain our ship, and you would still have me walk one of my loyal shipmates off the plank?"*

Patrick took a deep breath and continued, *"This is absurd,"* he sighed heavily, *"My God, it would be an easier task for me to walk the plank meself. It is indisputably to say that any of my men would willingly throw themselves in front of me at the sight of a menacing blade!"*

Patrick lowered his tone for the induced protocol he voiced next, *"You will have to forgive me, my Lord, but I cannot perform what is asked of me."*

Miguel knew he had hit an overly sensitive issue with Patrick, and the young Captain's outburst had indeed made him content. Patrick was undoubtedly loyal to his crew as they were to him. With his years of experience in the field, Miguel knew that loyalty among the crew was a crucial factor on a ship. It determined how long a captain stayed in command. Miguel, satisfied with Patrick's reaction, retracted his suggestion saying, *"No need for forgiveness lad, this was a logical solution for a merely greater pain in my butt, but with all the trust I've embedded in you, I will see fit that you acquire an alternate ... no* (clears his throat) *... the most desirable solution for my needs ... captain."*

Patrick was happy with the conclusion. He tried to hold back the smile that wanted to brighten up his chiseled face, but Miguel caught sight of it. He smiled back and patted Patrick on the cheek, declaring, *"A smart lad you are, and your crew is not alone to serve you revered. Now let us discuss a more serious matter at hand."*

"Fire away," Patrick sat down once again, attentive to his boss.

Miguel reached out for the letters resting on his desk, *"I have received three letters from our recipients that allege missing content in the cargo which we ... uh ... uh ... you ... delivered to them."* He paused to allow the news to sink in, *"These are serious allegations, and I do need to pose the question, do you have any wind of someone onboard your ship taking a personal interest in the cargo?"* Patrick was taken off guard regarding this allegation.

He definitely did not see this coming, because, in order for this to be true, someone on his crew was stealing cargo from the ship. With a perplexed expression, Patrick stated, *"At this moment I would have to disapprove of this allegation, I cannot think of anyone on my ship that would be capable of such an act."*

Miguel had three letters in his hands, which allegedly stated the wrong-doings, but being as wise as he was and can be, he concluded that this was not enough proof of the alleged wrong-doings, yet. So, he made a sane proposal, *"For the time being, this remains a simple allegation, which we need to act upon. And let us hope that this is not a little scheme coming from our, should we say, loyal and honest clientele. As an indication of our goodwill, I will order and pay for the missing merchandise, and we will have to ship the missing content to the rightful owners. But Patrick, this is a very serious matter, especially if it happens to be true. So, I ask of you to pay close attention to your cargo's inventory from this day on. Perhaps, you should think of appointing a trustworthy shipmate to aid you in this matter. Just make sure you choose wisely."*

Patrick could not agree more with Miguel. The recommendation was a logical one, and he accepted it as is. Miguel stood up, reaffirming their agreement, *"Very well then, if any wrong-doing is sited, I wish to be notified at once, aye?"*

Patrick nodded and replied, *"Aye, sir."*

Getting back to his ship, Patrick looked up towards the crow's nest and saw Knots climbing up the mainmast. To get Knots' attention, he puckered up to release a loud, strident whistle. Knots hears the sound and stopped climbing to look down at his Captain standing on the deck. He then grabbed a rope in front of him with one hand and flipped it sideways. Holding the rope behind his back, Knots waved back to his Captain, signaling a thumbs up to indicate that he was ready to set sail.

Patrick lifted his arm and motioned Knots with a repeated curling action of the finger, inviting him down onto the deck. Knots was at least thirty feet above the deck. Not sure if his Captain was indeed calling out to him, Knots pointed to himself with the hand holding the rope to confirm that he was the one who needed to come down. In doing so, as soon as his hand released the rope, Knots lost balance and started freefalling towards the deck.

"Knots, hold onto the rope," Patrick screamed, horrified of the possible implications of this fall, as he frantically ran towards the mainmast, not taking his eyes off the little man.

Knots swiftly turned his agile body around and grabbed hold of the rope to stop his descent, within a twelve-foot drop. He then looked down at Patrick's panic-stricken face, smiling sheepishly at him as he gave out another thumbs-up, saying, *"Good ... all good."*

Patrick breathed a sigh of relief, lowering his head to release some of the anxiety he had felt just moments before. Then it suddenly struck him; this was just another one of Knots' many tricks. Patrick couldn't help but smile at this lovable character who could sometimes give him a run for his money. He looked up at Knots, chuckled and clapped his hands to show his appreciation for the man's stunt.

Knots slid down the rest of the way and followed Patrick to the Captain's quarters. Once Knots walked into his office, Patrick closed the door behind him. Knots was always amazed by the richness of the Captain's quarters every time he walked inside it.

The quarter was elegantly appointed in a mixture of Dutch and English mahogany furniture that glared back at you whenever you stood close to it. There was always a fresh scent of citrus wax that made you feel like you were sitting in an orchard, and Knots loved that feeling. The modestly sized quarters opened into the Captain's office, which further had two doors in it. One of the doors led to his bedroom with all the fluffiness and comfort one could imagine, and the other opened into the dining room, which could have been easily called the glitter room, given the richness of its silverware. Patrick would always bring Knots into the dining room and have him pick a fruit from the fruit bowl whenever they discussed different matters. Knots never really had a clue about what the Captain was discussing, and Patrick was well aware of that. Knots would simply enjoy his fruit and make-believe he understood everything by nodding occasionally, which made his Captain laugh every time he did so.

Today, things were different. Patrick got straight to the point, talking about the little discussion he had with Miguel concerning the damaged sails, but Knots interrupted the discussion with a meaningful frown. Patrick realized he hadn't offered Knots any fruit today and explained, *"Sorry mate, fruit comes after the chat today. This is a serious matter which you need to understand,"* and continued to explain the damaged sails. Considering Knots did not understand a lot of English, he again had no clue what Patrick was trying to tell him. One word he did understand was 'sails.' So, he nudged Patrick's arm, took off the red bandana that was tied around his neck, and blew air into it to illustrate a sail – confirming he had gotten that much right.

"Aye," Patrick affirmed and pulled the cloth out of his hands to blow into it too. He soon realized that he would have to mimic most of the conversation in order for Knots to understand what he's trying to convey. Patrick started looking around his quarters for a piece of rope to illustrate a loose knot but didn't find one anywhere until he turned around and saw one around Knots' pants being used as a belt.

He approached Knots, grabbed both loose ends of the rope, a rope that once was probably a potato sack tie, and yanked it to untie the knot. Knots, alarmed, and puzzled at this gesture, grabbed his pants, and ran to the other side of the room. Patrick held one loose end of the rope, and as Knots sprinted away, this resulted in the entire length of the rope being pulled off his waist.

As Knots got to the other side of the mahogany dining table positioned in the middle of the dining room, he turned around to make sure he hadn't lost sight of his Captain. He was still baffled at his Captain's behavior – the frowns and the mumbling in Portuguese gave that away. Patrick didn't understand a single word Knots mumbled, but he was sure these were not pleasant ones. Patrick laughed at Knots. The look on his face made it crystal clear that Knots was getting an entirely wrong idea of what was going on here. Still laughing, Patrick invited Knots to get closer, but the shy little guy was still not convinced that everything was okay. Patrick had to tackle things differently to stop Knots from being skeptical about him and his intentions.

Stretching his hand out, Knots said, *"Gimme."* This was perhaps one of the few words in Knots' limited English dictionary that he had learned. Patrick walks closer to his crew member and couldn't help smiling at the very uncomfortable Knots backing away, repeating his words, *"Gimme; gimme."* Patrick stops midway and decides to mimic the event right away before Knots gets carried away with his hysteria. Patrick tells Knots to look at him by pointing Knots' eyes and then his own eyes.

Once Patrick was sure he had Knots' attention, he described his actions, *"Miguel ... big boss ... not happy,"* making a sad face. Knots nodded to confirm that he understood.

"Sails," He blew into the red cloth again, *"Knot ... no good,"* demonstrated a knot that came undone for Knots'

understanding. Knots confirmed his comprehension by nodding once again. It also dawned upon him that this discussion was not what he thought it was about.

Patrick continued, *"Knot no good uh-huh ... now sails no good,"* and tears Knots' red pirate-like cloth apart. Knots didn't like what Patrick had done to his neck cloth. It made him unhappy, and he frowned at Patrick to show disapproval over his action. Patrick giggled and apologized, before concluding, *"Sails no good ... Knots work no good."*

Knots understood. He hastily stomped past Patrick, grabbing his rope and torn cloth with one hand while holding his pants with the other. On his way out, he announced in a pronounced accent, *"Nuts (knots) nice now ... me do ... big boss happy ... me show you ... me have good nuts (knots)."*

It was clear to Patrick that Knots was intimidated, trying to get the phrase right, until he finally nailed it *"Me show now, big boss and you, me have nice nuts (knots),"* and quickly walked out the dining-room door. Knots' aggravation was obvious, so Patrick quickly offered him a fruit before he left the quarters, but Knots didn't waste any time and rushed out of the quarters determined to get the task right, or so Patrick hoped. Outside of the Captain's quarters,

Knot was tying the rope back around his waist when he hears, *"Do you need help with that little man. You wouldn't want to be losing ya trousers while running up thee mast ... hehe."*

Knots looked up, and there stood Brian, Patrick's first mate, smiling and staring down at him with his dark green eyes that refused to be overpowered by his bushy black eyebrows. There was sweat trickling down his face; it was a hot day. Knots did not understand a word the first mate uttered, but just by the way Brian grinned at him, he was certain that he was being mocked. Knots walked away to the side of the ship beside a wooden barrel to finish tying his pants while mumbling undefined words *"niania ... nianiania."*

Brian chuckled and replied, *"Nothin' a good night's sleep can't fix,"* as he entered the Captain's quarters.

"Aye captain, thee cargo's in place, and me lady is ready to embrace the sea one more time," Brian proudly announced, looking at Patrick end his laughter. His curiosity got the better of him, and he couldn't help but ask, *"Did you have a little quarrel with Knots?"*

"Not a quarrel, I simply needed to communicate Miguel's discontent concerning a few damaged goods," Patrick replies.

"That must have been quite the show and would explain his lack of humor too, but let me guess ... the sails?"

"A show indeed it was, and I'm convinced that he understood quite well. And aye, the sails were indeed the reason for our little chat. Miguel is at the end of his anchor with these damaged sails and would like to send Knots to the gulley."

Patrick paused before he continued the conversation, *"Miguel is also concerned about another matter, which is far more serious than the sails and I require another set of eyes to aid me with the investigation of this matter. One that I can trust will serve me well."*

Brian's reply came hypocritically when he said, *"And who might that be, me, captain?"*

Brian and Patrick had known each other since childhood. They were, without a doubt, the best of friends. Brian was quite similar to Patrick, only a bit shorter in height. They shared a similar build and tanned skin. Brian wore his light brown hair short, and his beautiful set of jade-colored green eyes would have women stare and swoon whenever a glance came their way. Brian had grown up as an only child, but sadly he had lost his mother to breast cancer at an early age. He was born in England but moved to Gibraltar, too young to have distinct memories of his mother, but every time he thought of her, it saddened him.

His father, Mr. Fuller, never bereaved the loss of his wife. As if that wasn't enough, he became an infantry, non-combatant soldier that was pulled out of the battle due to a severe injury to his leg. Mr. Fuller was known to be an incredibly happy person, but after these tragedies, his life took a turn for the worst, and Brian became the main target for soothing his deceptions.

Brian had always idolized Patrick like the big brother he never had but always wished for. He wanted to be just like him, and he was proud of him. His father, out of jealousy, never agreed to this friendship. He endlessly tried to separate his son from being a part of Patrick's life. Fortunately for Brian, he never had much success with that. Contrary to Mr. Fuller, Catherine just loved to see the boys together, because they always got along so well. They were also quite alike except that Brian had a hint of rebellion in him, which was certainly due to his father's never-ending cruelty. This drop of rebellion often brought him a bit of mischief, but even if trouble came walking to his doorstep, Patrick had a way of pulling him out of it every time. Brian often wondered how he managed to do so, but Patrick always had his ways.

Until this day, fate had kept them together, and Brian felt privileged to work with Patrick, especially as his first mate.

Patrick topped Brian's satirical question with some sarcasm of his own, *"I'll give you one chance to answer thee question mate ... and if you are wrong, I'll throw you overboard meself."*

Brian chuckled. He asked intriguingly, *"What does thee need me eyes fur?"*

"It has been said that some of our recipients have received cargo with missing content, and I will need you to help me ensure that the cargo is not manipulated before it reaches its destiny," Patrick replies. *"Tell me, Brian, do you have knowledge of such a man on board thee ship?"*

"Nay ... eh ... nay, I can't think of any mate on thy ship that is capable of such an act," Brian replied with a startled

look while shaking his head.

Brian's reaction seemed peculiar to Patrick, *"Very well,"* he replies, *"If ya see anything out of the ordinary, I should be informed at once. Do not take it upon yourself to justify any circumstance, and this discussion needs not to be discussed with anyone."*

Brian confirmed, *"Aye, sir."*

"Good. I believe we are ready to set sail?" asked Patrick.

"Right, you are captain," Brian replied enthusiastically.

"Jolly, you may give the word, destination Tangier," Patrick gave the command.

"Aye ... ly captain," Brian replied as he exited the Captain's quarter. Patrick left his quarters as well and headed to the helm to join his crew.

They set sail for Tangier, where fate was churning a plan of its own.

Chapter 3
A Day in the Market

On every beautiful sunny morning, the city of Gibraltar awakened to the sound of merchants busily preparing for their goods to be sold in the market place. The constant chatter and the friendly banter of the vendors would punctuate the morning air, announcing to the residents that a new day had dawned. This had been the city's custom for as long as the living memory of people could recall.

Walking through the bazaar, you would stumble upon a colorful assortment of vendors and merchants, all vying for your attention. A casual customer, if he entered the market, would be bombarded with shrill calls of any number of merchants, each appealing him to drop by *their* shop and get their merchandise which was *"fresher than fresh"* and always promised to be the best among the competition.

In that bazaar, you would find the bread merchant luring you in with the most delicious scent of freshly baked bread. If you kept walking, you would come across a sweet shop which sold honeyed rolls, a variety of pies, and puff pastries that you would find quite hard to resist. You would find merchants selling fresh apple, lemon, and watermelon juices to slake your thirst. The meat merchant would be hawking a variety of frozen meats in a big cool box covered with blocks of ice, though if you wanted to eat something fresher than frozen meat, you had the option of buying a fresh kill, too. You could do this by buying a chicken or a lamb in a little stable next to the cooler.

The stable was filled with all sorts of poultry: there were chickens, a fair amount of rabbits, and a few lambs, but during the holidays, like Christmas or Thanksgiving, the stable would be stacked with turkeys.

Right next to the stable, the bazaar had a dairy merchant who transported fresh milk, cheese, and eggs from the farm to his store daily.

The cloth merchants who sold lace and ribbons and calico, silk, and taffeta were another outstanding addition to this bazaar.

The merchants in the marketplace were immensely popular with the daily customers, and for a good reason. They never failed to provide what they needed and at a very good price. If you walked a bit further, around the paved brick road of the market, you would come across more merchants with larger, and eclectic products. Among them was a fish merchant who was the busiest on Fridays, various fruit vendors selling both exotic and ordinary fruits, spice and nuts vendor for those who were interested, a florist for those who had a dreamy disposition, and if you looked for him, you could even find a pasta merchant with a wide variety of homemade noodles, of all shapes and types, to satisfy your sudden craving for pasta. The marketplace had, for ages, served as a spot for women to gather and gossip.

The women would shop and, at the same time, exchange information about the recent happenings in their locality: for example, who had died, who had a wedding coming up, and which couple had their first baby in the last few days. The gossip mill ran like clockwork without any need for oil. Women alone could keep the engine of valid news and superfluous rumors running without a break. This is not to say that there weren't a lot of socializing options for menfolk in the market area; they had their pubs and taverns for entertainment. In fact, one was situated right on the next street, just east of the marketplace. The Green Sail Pub was a popular spot for the men who would convene and conduct their own gossips without being judged for it. It was a fact that one and all of them relished in consuming the reports of everything noteworthy that went down in the city. They saw it as a chance to put in their two cents and feel important for 'contributing' to the discussion.

Of course, men in a pub with a seemingly endless flow of alcohol at their disposal meant that things also often got out of hand. Their discussions would turn into disagreements, which then turned into brawls where fists were thrown, and abuses hurled recklessly, with complete freedom. This had happened so often that people grew accustomed and then immune to it.

Really, people thought nothing of it even when they saw men emerging out of the pub with their noses bloodied, eyes blackened, and tunics torn. Despite all the predictable chaos, the marketplace remained a site of enthusiastic civilian activity where most people met every day to keep up with the pace of the city. Observers went so far as to say that this little, tightknit social web was necessary for it gave lifeblood to the community of Gibraltar.

The marketplace wasn't just about the community's sole source of information but also a way of keeping their ties of kinship, friendship, and neighborhood strong. The importance of the marketplace as the central spot of the city became even more apparent on a day like today: the collection day. People knew that the marketplace would be filled with a deafening silence today. No calls would be heard, no laughter would pierce the air, and no commotion could be witnessed on this day that many dreaded.

The bell at the marketplace had tolled, announcing to everyone that the market was open, but like every other collection day, people could only make their purchases once the collection was over. This way, they could avoid the embarrassment of being ridiculed or targeted by the group that was feared by everyone in Gibraltar, a group they called the Hoodlums.

The Hoodlums were a little group of Spanish delinquents that went around terrorizing people. Their trade was to swindle people out of a portion of their hard-earned money through extortion and other intimidation tactics. They were also notorious for controlling the black market. This group was established during the last days of the war of the Spanish

Succession and was led by a man called El Camino, but nicknamed Garra Del Diablo, which is Spanish for the Devil's Claw. This man was a war profiteer who had made his fortune in the war, a time ripe for people like him to consolidate their power. At that time, understandably, everyone's attention was consumed by the war that raged on rather than by trivial local affairs. It had made it quite easy for El Camino to make the most of the unstable situation in the city and take control without being called to task by any authority.

His name suited him well, for he used fear as a weapon. He had also mastered the art of manipulation to a *"T."* So, you were definitely a victim caught in a devil's claw if you were ever unfortunate enough to catch his attention or be of any value to him in any way. He could compel you to give up your most prized possession and have you think that you made the right choice.

Those who knew El Camino's history recalled that he was the bastard son of pirate Juan Guartem, who had ravaged and plundered Panama's coasts in his heyday, but who was now better remembered for burning down the city of Chepo. Ashamed of being a bastard son of a buccaneer, El Camino had willingly, even gratefully, embraced the moniker bestowed on him by his followers. Today, his name is fearfully respected and acknowledged in hushed tones by all Gibraltar citizens whose fear of him had remained unparalleled and unchallenged for many years now.

Chapter 4
A Secret Known by All

Arriving at Tangier's port, Knots was waiting for the Captain's signal before ringing the bell above the crow's nest. This would announce their arrival and alert any traffic that they were entering the harbor. Patrick looked up at the crow's nest, nodded side to side while a grin set on the side of his cheek and said: *"Here we go."* He then stretched out his arm and showed Knots his thumbs up, giving him the confirmation to ring the bell and, at the same time, screamed out, *"Go ahead, Knots, let them vermin's know we're here!"* and chuckled.

The smallest of things amused Knots, and this was one of them. Knots, ready with the bell clapper's rope in hand, started swinging the rope from side to side while blowing in an old military metal whistle. Impatiently waiting for the moment to look proud, Knots did his job. He waved at people and gave directions to outgoing ships. Even though Knots took this task seriously and with enormous pride, others simply loved the show he put on while he was at it.

Patrick let the ship drift sideways towards the huge wooden dock between two smaller cargo ships already docked. Once the ship got close enough to the dock, Knots blew the metal whistle twice to signal the shipmates to hold back the ship using pushrods in order to avoid any damage to the ship, and of course, the dock. Once the ship was secured, both walkways were pushed off the ship, landing on the dock. Then the crew began preparing to get the cargo off the ship and onto the dock where it would wait for its rightful owner.

The ship was now secure. Patrick walked down the quarterdeck and saw Brian helping his men with one of the walkways. He approached him and said, *"When your men come up with the cargo, I want you to inspect all the merchandise coming off the bow side of the ship, I'll cover this side."*

Brian sighed in disagreement, and Patrick was puzzled with his reaction.

He asked, *"Do we have a problem here, mate?"*

Brian struggled a bit, then stood up, took off his cap, stretched his neck to Patrick's shoulder, and whispered:

"Ahmed's cargo will be coming through this side."

"And?" Patrick asked, raising his eyebrows.

Brian continued to whisper, *"And ... well ..."* He paused, crumpling his cap with his hands, nervous out of his wits, *"Sabah ... I mean, Ahmed has a special order which he needs me to deliver personally."*

"Ohhh ... I see." Patrick replied with a grin on his face. He looked at his crew that was also amused by Brian's struggle.*"*

"Tell me, did Ahmed request this himself?" Patrick spoke loud enough for the whole crew to listen in as he winked at them. They quickly understood that Brian had just opened the door for an unforgettable and merciless leg-pulling event, but he was too nervous to realize it. Boys will be boys!

"Aye ... eh n-nay, I thought I'd grant him this special service meself." He replied quickly, making up the excuse.

Patrick looked at him seriously, *"And what, may I ask, do I owe this privilege to?"*

Brian was at the end of his rope with excuses and was a little frustrated with having to answer to all of these questions, but as he stood up to affirm himself with the truth, which was most probably the only way to acquire an agreement at this point, Patrick held up his hand inciting Brian to stop. He turned to his crew and mentioned, *"Gentlemen ... wouldn't it be appropriate to serve a privileged client with a freshly bathed member of our crew?"*

"Aye Aye captain!" The crew responded in agreement.

"It would be shameful to settle for anything less, me lord, Captain," One of the crew members shouted with a big smile on his face.

Brian sighed.

He had a strong feeling that he was being played. As expected, Patrick grinned and looked at his crew, who were standing near the walkway. He pointed towards Brian with a nudge of his head. The crew understood his order, and four of them quickly grabbed Brian. They lifted him up and began walking towards the other side of the ship. While being carried away, Brian bellowed, *"Patrick ... don't you dare!"*

Brian struggled, but he was helpless. He continued to threaten Patrick even though he knew it was of no use.

"Patrick ... I swear ... I will kill you!" he had everyone's attention now. His voice became louder by the time they had reached close to the ramp. Brian yelled one last time, *"Paaatrrrrickk,"* before he splashed loudly in the water.

Knots, still in the crow's nest, heard Brian's scream, which gave him just enough time to see Brian fall into the water. Patrick laughed his way to the other side of the ship. Meanwhile, Knots came swooping down the main mast and jumped down next to Patrick to get a closer look at Brian drenched and swearing while swimming back to the shore.

Knots was often Brian's target for a prank, and Knots was simply enjoying every moment of this event. Patrick, still laughing, leaning on the ramp to see Brian.

"Captain my arse!" Brian avoided Patrick as he finally found the ground beneath his feet and began walking ashore.

Patrick looked at Knots and said, *"Here's a chance to even some scores matey, throw him a bar of soap."* Without hesitation, Knots ran into the Captain's quarters and came out with a big brand-new bar of soap. He held it in front of Patrick. *"No, no, no, you throw it at him and don't miss ye target,"* Patrick explained to Knots while making necessary gestures so Knots would understand.

Knots paused and looked at the big bar of soap, and a thought crossed his mind, *"if I break this bar of soap, I'll be able to throw several pieces."*

He threw the bar of soap to the ground, breaking it into several pieces, picked up all the pieces, and solemnly began throwing the chunks at Brian. Of course, Brian turned around to see where this was coming from and as the first piece of soap struck his head, Brian threatened Knots,

"Knots ... I am going to boot ya sorry dwarven arse. Just wait matey."

Knots understood most of the bad words that were said on the ship, so he knew what Brian's words meant. Frowning, he threw the remaining chunks of soap, but this time, he aimed them directly at Brian with a lot of aggression. The first one was a misfire but on his second attempt, Patrick roared with laughter when the chunk caught Brian in the back of the head for a second time.

Knots was surprised by his own aim. He knew Brian must be really pissed by now and would do something nasty to get back at him. Knots, without wasting any time, ran back up the main mast to the crow's nest and kept an eye out for Brian. Finally, Brian jumped back onto the ship with a look of vengeance. Patrick looked at his men and nudged his head again towards Brian while he walked on board. Two members of the crew grabbed Brian again, but this time in a friendly manner. Patrick came close to Brian. *"Now, I do believe we have the proper mate, freshly bathed, to serve our most privileged clientele."*

The members of the crew laughed while Patrick nodded, signaling his men to let go of Brian. He then put his arm around Brian and said: *"A fresh change of clothing would be most appropriate for a loved one, wouldn't you agree?"* Brian nodded in agreement and chuckled, even though he did not appreciate the prank, but replied. *"You know this doesn't end here, friend."* Patrick grinned,

"I suppose not," He replied icily.

"On a different note," Patrick continued, *"make sure the cargo has been inspected before you leave."*

Patrick let go of Brian as he made his way to the stairway that led to his room below the deck. *"Brian?"* Patrick was still waiting for Brian to acknowledge his order. Speaking over his shoulder, *"Aye ... got it ... inspect cargo then go."*

"Wonderful, the lad has a good sense of humor after all. Now, everyone back to work, our customers are in desperate need of their merchandise, carry on," Patrick ordered.

Patrick and the company always had a lot of fun with Brian when it came to Ahmed's cargo, and there was a reason for it. The reason for his special care was called *"Sabah,"* Ahmed's daughter.

Sabah was a bit younger than Brian and had a typical Moroccan façade. She was not very tall, but she had long brown hair that slightly tickled her shoulders. Sabah was a pretty face indeed, with dark chocolate eyes and slightly tanned soft skin. She was the only child in her family born and raised in Tangier. In an effort to substitute for the son her father never had, she worked very hard in the marketplace and enjoyed working with her father.

She was very energetic but soft at heart and often added a feminine touch to all her surroundings. It should be said that when needed, she had no problems crossing borders. In this life, her heart belonged to Brian. She would always be amused with his unsuccessful attempts at approaching her.

Nevertheless, she was ready to wait until he plucked up the courage to come forward and conquer her heart once and for all.

On the other hand, Brian's plan was to privilege Ahmed by personally taking care of his merchandise in order to gain access to his daughter – even if the effort granted him just a short period with Sabah. To this day, Brian had put enormous efforts into getting close to Sabah, and those efforts had always worked well for him. However, there was only one little problem. Brian never built enough courage to open himself up to Sabah.

Every time he would convince himself to do so, he would bail out at the last minute due to his lack of courage and self-confidence. This was a constant struggle for Brian, one that he would have to overcome for him to be where he wanted to be. However, one would wonder why such a struggle existed because Sabah, like Brian's shipmates and everyone else around him, was quite aware of his attraction towards her. She had never shown any signs of restraint.

Brian, alone below deck, said to himself, *"Today is the day, no backing out like the last time,"* while slipping on his shirt.

"Enough of this nonsense, lad!" He spoke to himself, breathing out hard. *"We need to do this,"* He said, still talking to himself as he looked into a deformed mirror to comb his hair. Greatly confident, he looked at himself in the mirror for the last time and said, *"Off we go, we can't keep the damsel waiting forever."* and walked towards the stairs and onto the main deck.

Patrick inspected his side of the cargo and signaled his men standing on the walkway to take the cargo to the dock. He turned around and saw Brian walking towards the cargo on the bow side. He broke into a run as he made his way to Brian.

"Brian ... mate, no hard feelings, I hope." He said out loud when he was in his earshot.

"I'm still debating if I should have any feelings at all," Brian replied. Patrick laughed out…

"Note taken, dear friend. But this might cheer ye up.". Patrick explained. *"I've taken the liberty to inspect the cargo on the bow side, and I've confirmed that the orders are very much complete."*

"You do trust me, don't you?" Brian sighed and frowned.

Patrick replied to Brian's gesture while nodding his head in agreement, *"Okay, well, you might not want to answer that right now, maybe later, huh."* Patrick said again, *"So there's no need to inspect the cargo, and you may proceed ...*" Patrick cleared his throat,

"With Ahmed's cargo." Brian completed his sentence with a straight face and replied. *"Well, well, I just might be able to forgive you after all ... Captain."* He added as he descended the walkway to the dock.

Looking through the merchandise on the dock, Brian picked up a few articles from Ahmed's stock and waved to Patrick, signaling that he was on his way to the marketplace. Once he arrived there, he would be announcing to most of their clientele that their merchandise was ready for pick up at the dock.

Brian was sprinting away from the ship, finally glad to be on his way. He had gotten about a thousand feet ahead when he heard Patrick call out his name, asking him to come back. Brian stopped and made his way back to the ship, quite annoyed. While approaching the ship, he noticed that all his shipmates were looking at him, walking back, which felt awkward.

Once he got close to the dock's merchandise, Patrick asked him if he had seen certain articles that were missing. Brian fumed, *"Captain ... really!"* He stretched out his hand to reveal the merchandise he was carrying and asked, *"Is this ye missing merchandise?"*

"Iy ... it is!" Patrick replied.

"I took a few articles out of stock to deliver them to Ahmed me self," Brian explained impatiently.

"Okay, if that's the case, everything is fine," Patrick replied, sounding relieved. He then whispered to Brian, *"You know, we have a thief on board, and I'm just making sure the cargo is all there."* Brian gave Patrick a sarcastic smirk and turned around to make his way to the marketplace again. As Brian began walking away, he heard the crew laugh their hearts out behind him. He realized he had just become the victim of another one of their pranks.

A few minutes later, Brian was finally on his way to the marketplace, and his nerves seemed like they would explode any second. Whether it was because of anxiety or nervousness, at this point, he couldn't tell. He arrived at the marketplace and saluted to all the merchants he met in the market. He informed them about their merchandise, but as he got closer to Ahmed's store, he realized that Ahmed was nowhere to be seen. This was unusual because he would always be outside talking to merchants or serving his customers. In a way, it made Brian incredibly happy and relieved. He wouldn't have to find an excuse to speak to Sabah now.

Without her father's presence, his encounter with her would be much easier to deal with. He finally reached the shop, and Ahmed was still nowhere in sight. He made his way through the doorway and placed the articles on an old wooden counter, making sure to make enough noise to draw her attention. He assumed that Sabah was somewhere in the backroom and would notice that there was someone in the store.

Brian's heart was racing with anxiety and waiting for her arrival felt like waiting forever. At the sound of light-footed footsteps. Brian was extremely uncomfortable, so he pulled off his cap and waved it in front of his face thinking to himself, *"Here she comes, get ready, don't screw this up."*

Sabah finally came out of the hallway, and the minute she saw Brian, she walked towards the counter while wiping her hands on her apron without losing a minute.

"Hey, Brian!" She greeted him with a smile on her face that was as radiant as the sun showing him that she was incredibly pleased to see him. It was as if the world had come to a stop for both of them. Brian's heart was racing at the speed of a lightning bolt as he tried to look calm.

"Hey Sabah," he replied, and in doing so, he reached out to shake her hand in a manner of greeting but out of nervousness, struck most of the articles he had placed on the counter, sending them flying and crashing to the floor.

He walked to the other side of the counter and excused himself for being clumsy *"I am sorry, really sorry me lady, I'll clean my mess."* Sabah giggled and helped him pick up the articles telling him that everything was fine. But once they were done picking up the articles, Brian noticed that they were standing awfully close to each other and realized that this would be the perfect moment to share his feelings with her.

Now was the time.

But unfortunately for Brian, when the articles had fallen to the floor, it made a lot of noise and alerted Ahmed's attention, which was talking to another merchant on the other side of the store. Brian had found the courage to discuss his feelings with Sabah, but Ahmed came walking through the door saying, *"Asalam,"* to Brian. Brian, who was incredibly nervous and feeling out of place, stuttered, *"A ... A ... Asalam,"* and out of respect for Ahmed, rushed back to where he had been standing before, on the other side of the counter.

Like most people who knew Brian, Ahmed also saw the glitter in his eyes every time he looked at his daughter. It was very amusing for Ahmed to see Brian, going to so much trouble to hide his feelings only because he liked Brian. He could also recognize all the happiness and joy he brought to his daughter when she was in his presence.

As Brian left, Ahmed felt a bit sorry for Brian. Ahmed knew how it felt to be in love and decided to help Brian without showing him or his daughter that he was aware of how they felt about each other.

Brian had only gone a few paces when Ahmed decided to call on him. He asked Brian for a favor and told him to go to the back of his store to get a couple of wooden crates so he could make a showcase in front of the store. Brian understood what Ahmed needed. He headed to the back of the store, but while he crossed the door, he heard Ahmed asking Sabah to go with him in case he needed any help. Brian said to himself, *"This can't be happening,"* but continued towards the back of the store anyway because Ahmed had asked him for a favor.

Alone, at last, this was the moment he had long-awaited, but Brian could not get his senses together. Sabah watched him go through the crates as if he wanted to avoid her. He was behaving as if she wasn't even there. She felt his nervousness and laughed lightly to calm him down. He finally found a couple of crates that would be perfect for a showcase and still not thinking straight; he gave them to Sabah and asked her to bring them to her father. Sabah picked up both crates, but they were very heavy.

As she struggled her way to the back door, Brian watched her leave. He realized that this was the time to share his feelings with her, or he probably would never get another chance like this again. He asked Sabah to stop where she was. But he asked her not to turn around. Sabah heard him and did exactly what he asked, but the crates were getting heavier by the second. Not being very specific, he told her that he had been trying to tell her something for a long time. In an attempted to tell her how much he loved her, the words refused to come out of his mouth for some reason. His nerves weren't supporting him either as he uttered something that made no sense.

Sabah had waited long enough for this moment, and she was not going to let it go to waste. She couldn't hold onto the crates any longer either, so she dropped them on the floor, turned around and jumped into Brian's arms. Sabah looked at Brian and said yes to everything that he was about to say. In the next moment, she kissed him and expressed all the love that she had felt for him, as he had felt for her.

The crates had created quite a lot of commotion when Sabah dropped them. Ahmed rushed to the back of the store when he heard the noise to see if everything was fine. As he got to the back door, he saw Sabah kissing Brian endlessly. Ahmed backed away from the door and looked up to God to give them their blessing.

In the next moment, thinking as the religious person he was, he had to find a way to stop this without alarming them too much and especially in a way that they wouldn't feel too uncomfortable. He took a quick look around the room and saw some bottles on the floor and kicked them. The noise broke them apart. Sabah got to the crates. Ahmed appeared in front of the back door asking the children if everything was alright. Ahmed respected them a lot and was not going to let this little secret come out. However, he looked at Brian disapprovingly when he saw Sabah trying to pick up the crates. Brian understood that look really fast and quickly told Sabah that he would bring the crates to the front.

Brian deposited the crates outside where Ahmed had asked him to put them. At the same time, one of the merchants stopped in front of Ahmed's store with his horse and carriage. He asked Ahmed if he wanted to go down to the port to pick up their merchandise. He looked at Brian and also offered him a ride back to the port. Brian asked Ahmed if he would rather have him stay to help with more work while he was at the port. Ahmed looked at Brian with a solemn look on his face saying, *"I think you have worked enough for me for one day."*

Brian had to agree, so they both got onto the carriage and headed for the ship.

Chapter 5
Fatima & Layla

Far away from Tangier, that same morning, Fatima, with her older sister Layla, had been strolling the marketplace in a Moroccan village named Fez.

It was yet another boisterous day at the market. Like most of the other marketplaces in Fez, which the locals called bazaars, it had been bustling with customers and buyers. The bazaars held great importance for the villagers, who would visit the many stalls searching for their desired merchandise.

Fez's marketplace resembled a visual fairytale, enriched with surreal colors and shapes – the throbbing mercantile heart of the village. It wouldn't be wrong to say that the merchants were proud of their merchandise, exhibiting them like each stall added to a fashion event for food – just a little tactic to tempt the people to buy more. Their efforts were not in vain for many people who hadn't even planned on buying anything ending up spending their money on them. The vegetables here were so colorful and just in the perfect shape. It was as if someone had painted them on a canvas.

The fruits too glared at you as if each one of them had been waxed the day before. The almond nuts mounted like pyramids looked mesmerizing. It blocked the sun so that the passersby would lay under its shade. It was a sight to witness it all with the naked eye for literally every person living in Fez.

In the marketplace, you could not tell the difference between who was who. The rich and poor, all frequented regularly. Everybody just mixed so well together in the marketplace as if they were a great big family, but there would be a few exceptions here and there. The bazaars were a lively place for the kids to run and sneak around too. They would slip candies into their pockets and tie firecrackers at the end of vendors' *shalwars,* and so on.

The marketplace was also about meeting people and talking about all kinds of stories. It was a place to chat, gossip, make and hear about rumors, out of which only some were true. Anyone could relate to the fact that it was the best place to hear about everything without meaning something personal to others. The sisters had been born in Fez, but both had contrasting personalities. They lived together, but Fatima, currently a widow, worked as the housemaid for

Layla along with Hanane, who was their cousin. Together, they were taking care of Layla's daughters, in which they both had no guilt in doing. Although Fatima had a much more blossoming personality than her naive sister. When it came to finding the right match for herself, she wasn't very lucky. Fatima knew that marriage was something she had to get done, sooner rather than later, given the incessant pressure from her family.

A while back, Fatima had married a Portuguese man while in her late teens. Portuguese men were allured by the intense beauty of sun-kissed looking, and gorgeous Moroccan women, but lacked in respecting their wives. Her late husband did fit the stereotype. He was a violent person and wouldn't think twice before beating, kicking, and assaulting her.

He did that only to satisfy his ego, nothing more. For him, it was about exerting power and control over Fatima. This was quite terrifying for her and tore her heart apart. Despite going through such domestic violence, she was a very loyal wife and tried to keep the knowledge of her husband's aggressive nature to herself. When she had married him, Fatima prohibited herself from saying anything against her husband, for she feared the consequences of her husband finding out about it. Fatima did not want to make her life more complicated than it already was. Thus, she would only discuss with others what was good about him. This way, everyone would believe she had a happy marriage. After all, not everyone has the propensity to comprehend the sorrow hidden behind jolly eyes.

She endured her husband's unjust attitude for nearly six years. As luck would have it, her husband died just before the seventh year of their marriage. Her husband had fallen off the boat somehow while net fishing, got caught in one of the fishing nets and drowned. Since then, she was living with her sister Layla who never stopped bringing rich men to the house to pair them up with Fatima.

Layla had desperately hoped that Fatima would get married to one of them as soon as possible and erase the awful memories of her late husband. Little did she know, it was easier said than done. Layla had no success in the two years she tried. Fatima, who was now in her late twenties, had no luck in finding the right man. But Fatima was having the time of her life in the absence of someone who would sexually, physically, and mentally abuse her. She knew that what she had with her late husband wasn't something she wanted to be a part of anymore.

Yet, it was not like she hadn't been looking for the ideal man.

After becoming a widow, all she looked for in men were that they would offer her respect, appreciation, and love her for who she was – she wanted everything she had been deprived of for all of her married years. Fatima was just waiting for the right man and the right moment. A moment when her heart would skip a beat for the ideal man while having butterflies flying around in her stomach.

Sooner or later, the right time will come, Fatima assured herself. She wouldn't hesitate to spend her whole life waiting for what she calls *"real love."* Her radiant blonde hair, eyes dipped in honey and blossoming, plumy cheeks, all added an exotic sheen of beauty to her humble and mesmerizing personality.

These were far from the features of a typical Moroccan girl, and her identity was often mistaken because of her looks, but she is, without a doubt, a genuine native Moroccan girl.

While Fatima trusted fate to bring her the awaited lover, Layla's case had already been closed by fate. She was a fortunate person to become a part of one of the privileged residents of Fez through her marriage with a local elite. She got married into the royal family after one of the members of a royal family got smitten by her. Layla didn't have to do much to live a wealthy exotic life of a Royal. Her luck did most of the work for her.

Although Layla was equally exquisite-looking as her sister and had a heart of gold, her lust for money took a toll over her other personality traits. Money grew to become everything for her. Since she became a part of the royal family, she inhabited an attitude that never really benefited her. It even made people despise her. For this reason, she usually had a hard time connecting with people and have a good time with them.

Unlike Fatima, Layla was a materialistic woman, the type of person who thought she had and knew everything, even though all her privileges were thanks to her husband's riches. This was precisely why she desired that Fatima too marry into one of the affluent households. *"That way, all your problems in life would vanish,"* she would say. Yet, she made special efforts to ensure that Fatima's suitors were not as wealthy. The way Layla thought about herself and others made her conceited. Due to the privileges, her luck bestowed to her, she came to believe that she was the next best thing to God. She lacked empathy and virtue. The only decent quality she had was her brimming motherly love for her two daughters. She would do anything to make them happy.

Fatima did not have any interest in the rich and the elites. She yearned for a man with personality. That was her prime need. She was happy to be working as her sister's housemaid, which, in itself, was a comparative privilege. But that favor was barely contributed to why Fatima loved Layla; her love was unconditional. Sometimes too unconditional, for it made her oblivious to her sister's schemes. That said, she was fully aware of her sister's vanity.

It was another bright, sunny day for Fatima in the bazaar, where at one point, she swerved from her sister to wander off alone. Soon, she found herself by the fruit vendors, surrounded by sweet scents and voices screaming, *"a dozen quinces for a dirham,"* or *"delicious savory tangerines, come and buy, come and buy."* She began picking out some apples to take back to her sister's little palace and as she handed the merchant his coins, a little quarrel distracted her. The sounds coming from behind her made her head turn towards them. A familiar voice had made her ears perk up, and she slowly approached the crowd. When she riffled past the many shoulders of gathered people, she found her sister Layla to be the main attraction of the quarrel. It wasn't anything new for her to witness. She was barely fazed at all. Layla has always been a problem child, and Fatima could not think of the last time she went out somewhere with her sister without her getting into a quarrel with someone.

"My sister and her royal attitude, God!" Fatima was mature enough to understand that someone from the Moroccan monarchy ought not to behave in the way her sister does. But it wasn't only Fatima who had seen a negative change in Layla's attitude and lifestyle after the royal marriage.

The way Layla used to argue on petty things made it evident to other residents of Fez that she was a spoiled individual with a sharp tongue. Many had noticed the downfall of Layla's personality before and after her marriage into royalty. Layla did not spare a single person when it came to exerting her power and superiority. She made a big deal over every little thing in public, especially in the marketplace. She considered even the vendors shabby and much deplorable in general. When it came to beggars, though ... At present, her poor victim was a beggar who had been sitting in peace under the palm trees' shade. His only sin was having his foot placed in Layla's path while he had lain half-asleep. That was enough to make the elder sister erupt. When Fatima got a hold of the disagreement, she walked right into the quarrel. No one else could have dared to if truth be told.

Layla left no chance to belittle the poor human, right in front of everyone, and they soon became the center of attraction. She was so wrathful, so engrossed in the argument that she had no idea that her quarrel was audible enough for everyone to hear.

If the quarrel were happening between the beggar and someone who did not belong to the royal family, no one would be interested. But people did not want to miss out on this quarrel. Perhaps there was an odd universal pleasure in witnessing the humiliation of a weak person by an elite. This would feed the gossip channel for at least a week, perhaps. For Fatima, this wasn't a pleasing moment to wait out. Layla being disrespectful to a beggar in the market showed an enormous lack of maturity, manners, and etiquette for a Royal Lady. But there she was, her face red-hot. Smoke may as well had been steaming from her ears. And when she was done arguing with the beggar, she spat on him and moved forward as if nothing happened.

This all happened just before Fatima reached her. She immediately regretted that she did not hasten. She couldn't care less about the reason behind the quarrel, but what her sister did to the beggar enraged her. Fatima was habitual of seeing her sister's rude behavior towards almost everyone. Be it maids, other family members, or people who do not belong to the royal family.

Nevertheless, she hadn't expected her to spit on someone, and that, to a beggar in a public place. She was more ashamed of her sister's behavior than ever. To compensate for what her sister did to the poor man, she untied the little scarf she had around her neck and wiped the spit off the beggar while mumbling soft apologies. It was the least she could do. The long-haired squalid beggar couldn't bring his eyes off the ground, given the humiliation he felt. He yet appreciated Fatima's gesture.

There must have been something about her that he did not even flinch when she had neared and touched him. He did not know who Fatima was and why she was so nice to him. Being completely oblivious about the fact that Fatima was Layla's sister, he thanked her many times. Surrounded by the crowd, while trying to clean her sister's saliva off the beggar, he grabbed her hand and softly told Fatima that everything was okay. Then he turned his face to watch Layla leave the scene.

The way he was looking in her direction made Fatima realize that he was never going to forget who this person was. After Fatima was done, the beggar bowed his head and politely offered his gratitude. He recited a gentle prayer and then said a few foreign words in a husky voice that Fatima could not understand. While doing so, he stood up and walked away at a leisurely pace.

Fatima was out of words and didn't know how to respond. She yet had this strange feeling that a beggar had blessed her. Oddly, she also felt they would meet again someday. Fatima was content for doing the right thing. If she had a chance, she would have apologized to him on her sister's behalf. Fatima looked over her shoulders to find the crowd behind her dispersed. Then she looked ahead at the beggar again and in an instant, he was surrounded by a herd of children with mud-smeared faces wearing torn clothes. One of the boys called him, *"Moustapha,"* with so much cheerfulness that it brought a smile on Fatima's lips. She realized that he must be admired and respected by poor children in Fez.

How elderly it had been of him not to say a word back to Layla, she thought. Although extremely diplomatic, Fatima knew how much Layla despised the presence of beggars who did nothing but sit around the marketplace all day long which made this quarrel practically unavoidable.

Fatima stood up and started walking in Layla's direction thinking that she might want to catch up to Layla before losing her in the crowd, or, she could always listen for the next quarrel and Fatima would find her sister just as well.

Chapter 6
Backing Out

After a few days of trades and delivering merchandise to many ports tied to the Mediterranean Sea, the boys were back home as the cargo ship inched closer to the banks of Gibraltar. The city has been a strategic gateway as it lies between the continents of Africa and Europe.

The ship came to a halt next to the port with a loud thud. Two members of the crew used ropes to tie the ship to the docks. The others got busy with their duties, duties that the captain had assigned to them. As per the instructions given to them, they made all the necessary preparations before getting off the ship so they could accumulate a little free time before sailing out the following morning.

All the valuables on board had to be taken off the ship and locked inside Miguel's secure storage cellars. The food and other rations had to be stored carefully in the cabinets inside the kitchen. All the merchandise had to be checked according to a list. The items were then locked in the storage area in the ship's hull if the trade goods were export items.

Import items were sent to Miguel's storage units and livestock needed to be taken to the stable. Patrick's crew had been on the ship long enough to carry out their respective duties without being told. These were tasks that they had to oversee each time they would sail back home, to Gibraltar. That day wasn't any different than the others. The ship was tied, and the crewmen were ready to leave after completing their chores when suddenly they all stopped midway.

They were surprised to see that Brian was still on the ship. There wasn't a trace of excitement on his face like there usually was and Brian was always the first one to leave the ship. He would be the most enthusiastic of them all at the aspect of getting off the ship and exploring the city. Brian wouldn't spend an additional second on the ship once they would reach their destination.

There were times when he would tiptoe off the ship when no one was looking. Brian loved going to the Green Sail Pub that was near the port. He would spend time with his friends and stay there till the late hours of the night. However, that day was different. Brian had recently been assigned to look after the merchandise. This was why he was supposed to be the last crew member to get off the ship. Miguel had complete faith in him, and Brian was aware of that. He had proven himself as someone who could be trusted with something as important as that. *"Brian, you are coming, right?"* one of the men asked him just before leaving. *"Iy, I will see you all at the pub. You carry on,"* he replied without looking at the crewman. *"Don't be late,"* he said and left. Brian was the only one on the ship.

It had been an hour after the sun had set beneath the Mediterranean Sea. The night sky was a shade of bluish-black. There was complete silence in the air except for the water and an occasional bird that would fly over the ship. It was almost 10 pm, and Brian still hadn't left. He kept glancing at his pocket watch and then towards the coastline. It appeared as if Brian was waiting for something to happen. He seemed nervous as he paced from one corner of the ship to the other. He had no clue about what he was going to do.

Brian looked at his watch again in anticipation. It was ten minutes past ten and he decided to get some rest. He had been on his feet all day and felt drained by then. He sat down right where he was standing on the deck and laid down. It was only a matter of seconds before Brian's eyes closed on their own.

Brian was about to drift off to sleep when he heard the sound of hooves hitting the ground. Brian immediately sat up, knowing that it was time. He saw a horse-drawn coach approaching the ship. Little did Brian know that he wasn't the only one who was woken up because of the horses. Knots was soundly sleeping in the crow's nest above the ship. He had been asleep during the entire time when the ship had reached Gibraltar. The sound of the horses dragging the coach behind them grew louder with every second. Knots sat up and peered from the crow's nest down to the ship.

Knots was surprised to see that Brian was still on the ship. Knots then looked at the coach that had stopped right in front of the ship's entrance. He then saw Brian straighten his clothes and walked off the ship. He made his way towards the stagecoach and stood near the door to greet the passengers.

The coach's door swung open, and the passengers stepped out one after the other. Knots cowered down and remained quiet. He didn't want Brian to know he was still on the ship. It was dark everywhere, but despite that, the moonlight was bright enough to make everything partly visible. Knots stood on his knees a little to get a better look at the men who had gotten out of the coach. With a bit of difficulty, Knots was able to recognize one of the men. Knot's eyes widened with surprise, the kind that sent a chill down his spine.

It was none other than Garra Del Diablo, also known as El Camino. The notorious leader of all the hooligans in Gibraltar. Knots was trying to figure out what was going on and why was Brian meeting Diablo, of all the people in the world. Diablo wasn't a man whom anyone would like to associate themselves with.

Knots had to know why Diablo was meeting Brian, and for that, he had to stay very still to avoid being seen by anyone. After all, he knew Diablo and what he was capable of. His reputation preceded him in every way imaginable. If Diablo saw Knots there or anyone else there for that matter, Diablo wouldn't think twice before throwing them in the sea.

Brian greeted Diablo and his men with a forced smile. He directed them towards the ship. He looked around to make sure no one could see them. Once he was sure, Brian led them inside the ship. Once everyone was on-board, Brian came and stood in front of Diablo. He was about to say something when Diablo raised his hand to tell him to stay quiet. He shot a look at the hoodlums, and within a split second, they dispersed in every corner of the ship. They stationed themselves on all the corners of the ship while two of them walked behind the stairs that led to the upper deck of the ship. Knots noticed how they didn't waste any time in going right where the crates were placed. Knots understood that this wasn't their first time on the ship. The hoodlums appeared from behind the stairs a couple of minutes later carrying two wooden crates. Inside was the merchandise that Miguel exported across the country. Brian didn't move or say a single word as the crates were brought out in front of him. He watched silently as Diablo's men got off the ship and placed them in the coach.

Knots couldn't believe his eyes as he witnessed Brian's indifference towards everything that was going on. Diablo was stealing from them, and Brian was letting him do it. While this was happening, Diablo rolled some tobacco on a sheet of paper and lit it up. He puffed out rings of smoke while his men did all the work for him. The air began to reek of old tobacco and spirits. Even Knots could smell it all the way up inside the crow's nest. Diablo flicked his cigarette butt over the ship. Brian heard a tiny fizzling out sound as the cigarette hit the surface of the water. Diablo reached inside his pocket and fished out a rolled-up wad of currency notes. He extended his hand towards Brian and held the money in front of him. Brian stood still for a few seconds, but then took the money and kept it in his trousers' pockets, much to Knots' dismay.

Diablo shot Brian a smirk and walked away. Knots could not believe what he had just seen. Brian was stealing from the ship and selling it to the hoodlums. "There has to be a good reason behind it," Knots thought.

Brian continued to look at Diablo as he walked towards the small ramp that they had used to get on the ship. Diablo was about to step down the ramp when Brian spoke. *"Wait,"* he said, loud enough so Diablo could hear him.

Diablo turned around and looked at Brian blankly.

"I need to talk to you. It's important," Brian began. *"What is it? Make it quick,"* Diablo said in his throaty voice.

"I am done. I don't think I can do it anymore," Brian said with bated breath. He wasn't sure what Diablo would do after hearing that, but he knew it was the right thing to do.

Several creases formed on Diablo's forehead as soon as Brian finished talking. Brian could tell he wasn't pleased by what he had just heard. Nonetheless, he remained quiet. Brian took it as an opportunity to go on. He exhaled and continued, *"I came to you because I was desperate, and there was no other way. I wanted the money because my father was sick, and he needed medical care. He's doing well now, so there's no reason for me to keep doing this. This isn't fair to Miguel or my fellow crewmen. They are my family, and the thought of betraying them keeps me up each night,"* Brian's voice cracked when he mentioned Miguel and the crew.

Knots heard everything that Brian had said to Diablo. He was worried about Brian. He was afraid Diablo might hurt him. Knots wanted to help Brian but was uncertain of what to do.

It wasn't wise what Brian did. He shouldn't have used his father as an excuse in a situation like that. Everyone was aware that Brian's father, Mr. Fuller, was an alcoholic who had wasted his life in a bottle.

Diablo's loud, merciless cackle broke the silence in the atmosphere. He was mocking Brian for his naivety.

Diablo stopped, and the laughter was replaced with an evil snarl. He looked at Brian and said, "*Listen, kid. Do you think this is a game? Just because you started, this doesn't mean you get to end it too. Things don't happen according to your convenience, boy. If you knew this would happen, you shouldn't have started this in the first place,*" Diablo spoke hoarsely. He mouthed each word like he was doing Brian a favor by talking to him. He stopped for a second and then continued.

"*You want to back out? Sure, go ahead. I will be happy to meet Miguel and tell him all about our little secret,*" and at that moment, Diablo saw the color drain from Brian's face.

Diablo let out another sinister sound of laughter before saying, "*Don't worry, kid. No one will find out. You will get used to it. It's a good deal for both of us. You're going to be a rich man very soon. Mark my words,* "He patted Brian's shoulder as a way of telling him to calm down.

"*I will see you soon,*" Diablo bade goodbye to Brian and left. Brian saw Diablo walk towards the coach and climb into it. His men followed him and were ready to leave on his orders. The horses neighed and galloped the same way as they had arrived. They stagecoach pulled away, and Brian couldn't help but think about the merchandise that was on it.

Knots was taking his time to process what he had just seen. He was having a hard time believing it all. He never took Brian for a thief who could betray the people he worked with and considered him a part of their family. Brian was one of the most trustworthy and honest guys that Knots had gotten to know during his time on the ship.

Knots had never seen Brian do anything that was remotely out of the line. To find out that he was in business with Diablo, a business that involved stealing from the ship was something that Knots had never imagined even in the wildest of his dreams.

Despite hating Brian for landing himself in a situation like that and for stealing from Miguel, Knots was certain that he wasn't going to say anything to anyone. Funny enough, Knots didn't want to get involved because he was afraid he would lose everything he had worked for in all these years. He had a job and a sense of direction, and he didn't want to lose any of that. Besides, he might lose his life if Diablo would find out that he had ratted out on him. Knots figured out that it would be wise for him to stay quiet.

Chapter 7
Mr. Fuller

Brian could see the hoodlums leave. He kept looking at them until they were out of sight. He wanted to make sure that they had left and weren't going to come back. As soon as they disappeared, Brian reached in his pocket to pull out the bag he put the currency notes in. He opened it and took a good look at the money inside. All of this had come from the merchandise that Brian had stolen from the ship. He sat down and didn't know what to do anymore. He tightened his bite, clenched his fists, and let out a loud scream of anguish.

Brian rose from the ground while clutching stacks of notes in both of his hands. He was hit with a sudden feeling of guilt and anger. Not knowing what else to do, he threw the wad of cash in the air.

The string fastened around the bills broke off, and the notes began flying all over the dock. Brian wanted to turn his back on it and walk away, but he knew that this would just lead to another unpleasant argument with his father, which he wanted to avoid at all costs.

Brian gathered all the bills and made his way home. He placed the key in the barrel, twisted the lock, and pulled open the door to find his father sitting in a chair waiting for him rather impatiently.

Any other father would have greeted his son and told him how much he was missed, and the sentiment would have been most probably returned, but that wasn't the case here. Mr. Fuller was no ordinary father. The moment Brian stepped inside the house, he began spewing his anger and bitterness on him.

"Where have you been?" he began. *"Let me guess ... at the Green Sail Pub again. And what did you do there? Pretended to be smart in front of other people, something that you're not? How puny. How reckless. Do you care about the duties and responsibilities that you have towards us, huh?"* he continued to hurl his words at him.

"I am certain that you will never grow up to be a responsible man," he huffed and puffed, and Brian knew what was about to come up next. *"When I was your age, I was already promoted as a corporal in the army. You should take a good look at yourself. You are still scouring worthless objects from a boot deck,"* Mr. Fuller concluded.

TWO LIVES TO A DESTINY

This was a daily ritual, a daily routine for Brian. He had gotten used to his father's spiteful words. Those were all that he ever got to hear from his father. Things have remained this way ever since Brian's mother passed away. Their relationship was never this bad. Brian enjoyed a happy family with his mom and dad. His relationship with his father used to be one of love and understanding. Their dynamics changed with his mother's death, which made his father cold, distant, and bitter.

Deep down in his heart, Brian knew that his father was a good man and loved him a lot. After the death of his wife, something broke in him to the point of no return. Little by little, Mr. Fuller started losing his kindness once the doctor's discovered Brian's mother had breast cancer. The doctors had performed a surgery to remove a primary infectious tumor, but further reports suggested that cancer had already seeped into the lungs through the lymph nodes. She died soon afterward because of what the doctors said was 'metastatic breast cancer.' Believing that the cancer was contagious, all their friends, family, relatives, and all those around them marked the Fuller family as quarantined. They decided to stay away from them to the point of isolation.

It had been a long time since she died, but Mr. Fuller still hasn't gotten over the loss of his wife. Both missed her dearly. Not a moment went by when they didn't think about her and didn't remember her in the little things she did.

Brian remembered that his mother was a virtuous woman who always believed in doing good by everyone around her. Perhaps that was why Brian loved Patrick's mother, for she reminded him of his own mother. Brian and Patrick had been together since they were kids, and Catherine had been like a mother to him, especially ever since he lost his own.

She had always treated Brian like her own son, just how a true mother would treat her child. But Brain's dad just needed to take his pain out on someone. Brian being the closest to kin meant he needed to accept his fate or move out.

Brian let go of his train of thought and asked his dad, *"Did you take your medicine? I kept them on the bedside table for you."*

Mr. Fuller's expression was still the same *"You're my son and not the other way round. Don't forget that, you don't tell me what to do,"* he proclaimed.

Brian had a lot going on in his mind. He didn't feel like dealing with his father's attitude at that moment and decided it was best to leave his father and retreat into his room. Brian could hear his father shrieking that he was a coward and didn't know how to have a proper conversation with his own father, but he chose not to reply. He closed the door behind him and drowned out his father's voice.

He walked towards his bed and laid down. Everything was finally quiet. He felt relieved knowing that there was no noise. The silence was a blessing for him at this point.

The days had become tougher and tougher for Brian and continued to go that way. A sea of problems whirled around him, and there was no way to get out of them. The only ray of light at the end of the tunnel was Sabah.

She was the only positive aspect of his life amidst all the negativity that surrounded him. She was the driving force in his life, which kept him motivated to stay alive and power through. Whenever he was in the face of adversity, he would close his eyes and try to picture Sabah's eyes that sparkled each time she saw him. Suddenly, Brian was yanked out of his thoughts by the dull thuds that suggested his father was approaching his room. He could sense him standing outside.

Mr. Fuller had had an exceptional career in the army, but it all came to a sudden halt when he was severely injured on the battlefield. The injury affected his behavior and the way he looked at life. Losing his wife in addition to this was simply the drop.

He knocked on Brian's door and walked in without waiting for Brian's permission. *"I need to talk to you. Come into the kitchen. I am waiting for you,"* he said calmly and left.

Brian was surprised, but he knew what it meant. Brian was sure that his dad was now embarrassed by the way he had behaved towards him. This happened all the time. Mr. Fuller would argue with Brian, and then after reflecting on his actions, he would realize his mistake.

Brian thought that this might be a good time to share something special and important with his father, now that he had returned to his senses. The news he had might actually make his father happy, he thought. Brian walked out of his room into the kitchen and sat in front of his father, who followed him with his usual motions. Mr. Fuller apologized for being rude and for reprimanding him needlessly. Brian comforted him in response and began telling him about the girl he met a while ago, and that he has also fallen in love with her. Mr. Fuller sat quietly, listening to the story without any expression of anger or irritability on his face. Brian figured that his father was happy about what he had shared with him.

He went on slowly revealing more details making sure that his father's temperament didn't explode for some reason or another. He assumed it would have happened by now if it had to, given how impulsive Mr. Fuller was. Luckily for Brian, things didn't seem to be going in that direction. He was happy to see that there was a genuine sign of happiness on his father's face and Brian was having a hard time processing this, but he seemed really happy with what Brian was telling him.

They continued talking to each other. It was one of those moments when neither of them was making an effort to talk. It was just flowing, and both were enjoying having this conversation with each other. As they kept discussing, Mr. Fuller gave him advice backed up by his own experiences with women. He kept chuckling as he recounted those experiences, which Brian mirrored with wonder. Things had not felt so smooth and free of turmoil between both of them for a long time. Brian was extremely grateful for this moment.

Mr. Fuller asked him, *"So son, when can your special friend come to visit us? I would like to meet her."*

Brian went silent for a couple of seconds. He then took a deep breath and said, *"It won't be possible at the moment, or anytime soon for that matter,"* he then launched into the more sensitive details of his situation.

He told his father that Sabah lived in Morocco. He also told him that it wouldn't be easy for them to be together, but that in no way did this mean it was impossible.

What Brian didn't know was that he was about to get a piece of his father's mind that he was still unaware of. As soon as Mr. Fuller found out that Brian's girlfriend was Moroccan, his expressions changed immediately.

He banged his hand on the table really hard and bellowed, *"Are you out of your mind? Or have you lost the ability to think for yourself?"*

Brian wasn't expecting such a reaction from him. He immediately realized his judgment was stemming from racist thoughts.

He continued, *"Have all the British girls died, or are they not good enough for you?"* his face was red with anger. *"Let me make this very clear to you, I will never allow a foreign slave in my house, no Moroccans, no Spaniards and definitely no Frenchmen,"* he concluded. Mr. Fuller had now reverted to his usual tirade, saying every vile, mean, and hurtful thing that crossed his mind. Each word was laced with more anger and hatred than the previous one. It went so far that even Brian began to feel humiliated, which was something he despised feeling. Despite it all, he remained calm and collected.

Brian would have remained silent, but it came to a point when Mr. Fuller started using offensive words against Sabah. He had never even met her, but she became a "manipulator" and a "villain" to him. Words that were not easy to forgive. Brian could feel every word prickling his skin like needles. One after another, he endured every word, but he was losing his patience. The discussion had taken a horrible turn, but Brian was unsure of what he was going to say next. His father, the ex-Army officer, was stamping over everyone that had ever walked the face of the Earth except the British – no surprises there. Only they were worthy of respect and no one else.

Mr. Fuller went on to say the most hurtful thing he could. He said, *"Wait a minute ... so is this where my hard-earned money goes? You are spending all of that on a tramp to impress her when you should be taking care of your ill father? What a son you are! I hope you burn in hell for this, I really do."*

As soon as Brian heard that, something broke inside him. Those words pierced his skin like someone had stabbed him with a knife. He knew that he wouldn't be able to take it any further.

Brian leaped from his seat and jumped on his father. He kicked his walking stick out of his hand and caught it before it fell to the ground. Mr. Fuller lost his balance and was about to fall when Brian grabbed him by his shirt and reached for his neck while jamming the hook of the stick near his mouth, making it impossible for him to speak.

He inched closer to his face angrily, glaring into his eyes, while the veins popped on his forearms.

"If burning in hell means I get to be away from you, I will welcome that with open arms. Hell would be bearable now

that I have spent my life living with you."

Brian didn't know what had gotten into him.

He continued, *"If you so much so utter a single word about the woman I love with that hate-filled, disgusting mouth of yours, so help me Jesus-Christ and all things holy, I will shove this stick down your throat to make sure nothing ever comes out of your mouth again."* he finished and loosened his grip on Mr. Fuller. The stick left his hand and bounced and clanked on the floor.

This was the first time that Mr. Fuller had seen Brian so angry. He was trembling. He felt like he had just stared right into the devil's eyes.

Brian let go of his shirt and stood back, still looking at his father with more bitterness than he had ever felt. He stuffed his hand in his front pocket and fished out all the money he had. He threw the wad on the table and yelled, *"There is your God right there. Worship it all you want."*

With that, he lifted his coat from the coat hanger and stomped out of the house, slamming the door so hard behind him that the windowpanes rattled for a couple of seconds.

Each time there was a disagreement at home, he went to the one place where he knew he would feel better and welcomed. Patrick's house provided him refuge, and that was where Brian headed.

Patrick had already changed into his sleepwear and was about to jump into bed when he heard a rap at the door. Startled because he was not expecting anyone, he hesitated for a moment and then wondered who was at his door at this hour.

He walked out of his room and yelled to his mother, *"I'm going to get the door. I think it's Brian."*

Catherine whispered, *"Oh my dear boy,"* under her breath. Patrick walked down the staircase and opened the door. He didn't even have to glance into the peephole.

The door opened, and there stood Brian. Patrick wasn't even surprised. He gestured him to come in. As Brian entered, Patrick shouted dramatically over his shoulder, *"Mom! Your beloved son has graced us with his presence. He will be spending the night in our humble abode,"* with a comical grimace. Patrick looked at Brian to see if this had made him laugh. Brian stood there with his head low and shoulders slumped. Patrick sighed and understood that Brian had another fight with his father.

Patrick asked him to come to the dining table, *"Let's talk here. I'll make some tea."*

Both walked towards the kitchen, but Brian didn't sit down until Patrick grabbed his shoulders and pushed him down to sit.

"So, what happened this time? What did you two argue about today?" Patrick began the conversation while filling the kettle with water and placing it on the woodstove.

Brian stayed quiet. He put his face in his hands and closed his eyes. All he could hear was the sound of Patrick fetching cups from the cabinet. Moments later, the kitchen was vitalized with the smell of fresh tea. Patrick didn't say anything after that until he sat down in front of Brian. Brian looked up when the smell of freshly brewed tea hit his nose from below.

Brian took a sip and looked at Patrick, *"This is really good. Thank you."*

"I know. Now tell me, what happened?" Patrick said again.

Brian recounted the salient points of the fight that he had just had with his father. This wasn't news to anyone, Brian would fight with his father, and then go to Patrick's place to vent off some steam. The reason for these arguments was usually the same. So much the same that Brian was tired of telling the same stories repeatedly. This time was no different, except for when he spoke about Sabah. Brian hashed out some of the details and then went quiet. He spoke with breaks about how he had fallen in love with Sabah.

Catherine walked into the kitchen and while pouring herself a glass of water. She overheard Brian recount his story and was just now learning about Sabah. She was surprised and interrupted the boys to ask more about Sabah. Brian loved how the discussion that ensued in that house was more pleasant than the one in his own home. Catherine hugged him and kissed him on the forehead then said, *"Brian, when you have some time on your hands, you should give a bit of advice to your captain so he may find someone like Sabah."* All three of them burst into laughter.

Catherine's words made Brian think of an idea. He was aware that Sabah was going to ask her father if he could attend an annual festival in Tangier. This was the right time to ask Patrick to accompany him to this festival. Every merchant in Tangier was familiar with Patrick and always had good things to say about him. But the real problem was more about Patrick being an introvert, and the annual festival meant only two things: socializing and people.

It didn't take him five seconds to say *"NO"* when Brian asked Patrick to accompany him. But Catherine hadn't spoken yet, and it seemed that Patrick needed a little convincing. Catherine was the kind of mother who never stopped her son from trying something different and exciting if that meant learning something new. She always encouraged him to go on adventures and welcome each learning opportunity with an open heart and mind. She knew that Patrick was a timid person, and she really wanted him to let go of that shyness and awkwardness.

Brian wanted the same thing for his best friend. Each time he would ask Patrick to go with him on a journey or an expedition like that, Patrick would say no. They both understood Patrick's caprice, but this time, neither Catherine nor Brian were having any of it. Catherine discussed and encouraged the outing with Brian as an ally and after Patrick forcefully accepted to accompany Brian, it was decided.

Both were going to this year's festival in Tangier, and Brian intended to make sure that it was a night that Patrick would never forget for the rest of his life.

Chapter 8
Meet & Greet

The year-end festival is one of the most exciting events of Tangier. People from all over Morocco come to Tangier to take part in the annual celebrations. This year, Sabah really wants Brian to attend it with her. For a while, she had known that Brian's ship would be at the port just when the festival would kick to its start. But Sabah needed her father's permission to invite her lover.

Her father, Ahmed, was in his shop. She decided to bring tea for him as an excuse to request his permission. She knocked on the shop's door, and Ahmed told her to come in. She placed a cup of tea on the table in front of him and stood there. He noticed she had not moved from her place.

"All okay, dear?" Ahmed asked.

"I needed to ask you something, father," she said.

"Yes? what is it?" he asked

"I wanted to ask you if I could invite Brian and Patrick to the festival?"

She mentioned Patrick's name and Brian's because she didn't want him to suspect that she had feelings for Brian. Little did she know, Ahmed knew already how she felt about Brian. He didn't refuse.

"Oh, of course, that will be great. You must invite them," Ahmed said, thinking it would be fun to have the two boys around for the festival. He resumed his work, and Sabah stepped out of the shop with a smile on her face.

Sabah met Patrick and Brian two days later and invited them. Brian and Patrick, having already discussed it, accepted her invitation right away. They were as elated as if they had been bestowed with an esteemed honor.

On the day of the festival, both Brian and Patrick reached the venue on time. They were hesitant at first to mingle around but eventually gelled in with the crowds. Ahmed joined them and began showing them around. He introduced Brian and Patrick to everyone with pride.

He knew them both very well and loved both of them as if they were his own sons. The feast began shortly after the introductions. Women dressed in traditional Moroccan attires of different hues began serving the food with friendly smiles. Moroccan people love their food and cuisine and are always incredibly grateful for all that has been given to them. Today is also a special day because they get to eat and share their food with the poor and the needy. The feast was followed by the tea of kings, better known as the Sultan tea. People relished the tea while exchanging exciting stories and anecdotes with each other.

Both Patrick and Brian enjoyed the food and fanciness, but the next part was going to prove a little tricky for the two. It was time to get up and dance. Musicians carrying their instruments placed themselves on what looked like a dance floor and proceeded with their symphonies. Soon the air was filled with sweet and soulful melodies of traditional Moroccan music.

Everyone got up on their feet and began swaying and dancing to the sounds of rubab, oud, kamenjah and tambourines. Sabah, who was looking exquisite, joined Ahmed, Brian, and Patrick at their table just as the dancing began. She and Brian kept exchanging glances with each other every now and then while Ahmed and Patrick were heavily engaged in a conversation. Shortly after, Sabah's cousins, Fatima and Hanane, walked in together from the entrance. They had traveled the entire day from Casablanca after visiting their aunt and were finally there to attend the festival. When Sabah caught a glance of them, she got up from her chair and went to greet them. Brian's eyes followed Sabah to see where she was going but Brian was sitting at an angle from where he couldn't see who she was greeting. Ahmed saw his concerned look and grinned. Brian, while trying to adjust his line of sight, saw Ahmed's grin and then grinned himself, knowing he had been made.

Ahmed got up from his seat and shouted, *"Let's dance"* and made his way slowly to the dance floor inviting the boys along with him. The musicians had decided to play a popular waltz, and Ahmed was confident that the boys knew how to dance to their genre of music. Both gentlemen suddenly grew very shy because neither of them knew how to dance.

Ahmed kept on posing gestures inviting them to the dance floor and the boys finally gave in and joined him. They stood there looking at everybody dance and then they looked at each other. They then shrugged their shoulders in a way that meant they had done much sillier things, and this couldn't be worse. Elderly wives and friends joined them with a giggle, and the boys began mimicking their footsteps as they started moving around slowly with the tune. Ahmed and everyone else encouraged and helped them one by one to show them how it was done. Everyone was moving around in circles, and each person would break away from the formation to join either of them to guide them.

Patrick and Brian got amazingly comfortable with the dance and began having a great time on the dance floor. Patrick swung around and surprised himself by staying in rhythm as he stretched out his hand and caught hold of his next partner. At this precise moment, his palm felt one of the softest hands he had ever held. Although he was extremely tempted to look up, he kept his focus on the dance and his eyes on the delicate feet moving gracefully in front of him.

Finally, he looked up at her, and just like in a dream everything slowed down and started moving slowly as his heart skipped a beat. His eyes were staring at the most beautiful girl he had ever seen. It was Fatima, Sabah's cousin. Like an anchored ship, Patrick couldn't take his eyes off of her. Patrick was so gazed that he wasn't able to see that Fatima was also going through a similar reaction. She had also realized she was dancing with a very handsome man and couldn't hide the blush that crept to her cheeks.

She tried to focus on his face but then lowered her eyes. Her attraction to him became too strong even though this was simply a glimpse in time. Neither paid any attention to their surroundings anymore. Time had frozen for only a few seconds but that's all it took for fate to set a new destiny for these two lives. A destiny to be considered one of the most powerful of all. One of "love".

The end of the piece but mostly the absence of music brought them back to real life. Although they were the only ones to share this encounter, Fatima felt like everyone around her saw it or even felt it. She glanced from here to there in awkwardness and then paced away to her table.

Patrick was still in a state of euphoria as he watched her go away. He still couldn't fathom what he had just felt. He had just danced with an angel. It was as if a spell had been cast on him. Brian hurried over to him and nearly dragged his friend off the dance floor.

He said, *"That was so much fun, Patrick. Did you enjoy dancing?"*

Patrick was still somewhere else. He wasn't paying any attention to what Brian was saying, so he just nodded.

Ahmed had witnessed Patrick's encounter with his niece and joked about it, *"Looks like Patrick just had the best dance of his life."*

Again, Patrick just shook his head without actually hearing anything. As he started to come back to reality, he kept scanning the place everywhere to find his little angel, but he couldn't find Fatima anywhere. Shaking his head, Brian asked Ahmed, *"Where is Sabah?"*

"Oh, yes, she reminded me to tell you that she went home. Fatima, the girl who danced with Patrick, was exhausted. Sabah took her cousins to our house. They have a long day tomorrow. They have to travel back home," Ahmed informed.

Upon hearing this discussion, Patrick's attention scrolled to Ahmed's words. He understood that Fatima was leaving tomorrow, taking his chance to meet her again.

Patrick heaved a disheartened sigh and clenched his fists tightly. Patrick's heart sank. He didn't know what to say or do, so he decided to call it a night and bid goodbye to everyone. He walked to the ship with heavy footsteps thinking a good long sleep would make everything better. He got on the ship and laid down on his bed without changing out of his festival clothes. He lay awake in his bed, thinking about Fatima while looking at the sky through his chamber's window. Brian walked in after a while and checked if Patrick was still awake. Patrick had heard him coming, but since he didn't feel like talking, he closed his eyes and pretended to be asleep. Brian found him sleeping, so he didn't make a sound. He quietly changed his clothes and got into his bed. He was exhausted and fell asleep quickly.

Patrick wanted to sleep, but he couldn't. Each time he would close his eyes, Fatima's face would appear before him. He couldn't stop thinking about how absolutely beautiful she was. He was delighted to meet her, but he was also a bit sad as he couldn't see her before she left Tangier and he probably wouldn't be able to see her anytime soon. He kept tossing and turning the entire night in his bed. These thoughts and fantasies kept him restless. Finally, he resolved to meet Fatima in the morning regardless of the situation and then fell asleep. The next morning, Patrick and his crew had to sail back home to Gibraltar. All Patrick wanted to do is to go to Ahmed's place and meet the lady who harassed his sleep the entire night, but he felt challenged by his responsibilities and decided otherwise. He did what he was supposed to do and assembled his crew. He executed his duties and made sure that his ship sailed on time. All of this was very difficult for him, but he still went ahead with it. Meanwhile, Fatima stood on the cliff directly in front of the port where Patrick's ship stood. She could see him standing on the front deck of the vessel in a bridge coat with a spyglass while other crew members scurried about, carrying out their duties. She reasoned that he was the captain and the one in charge. For Fatima, Patrick managing his crew was a splendid sight.

Like Patrick, she hadn't slept the entire night either and was restless to watch him cruise away. The anchors had been pulled in, and the ship began sailing on the calm waters. Fatima closed her eyes and prayed for Patrick's safe return so that she could soon meet the man she had set her heart for.

The ship had left the port, and Patrick was looking ahead when suddenly he felt he should turn around and look towards the back of the ship. He didn't know why, but he did, and sure enough, he could see a feminine silhouette standing on top of the cliff. He reached for his spyglass, but he couldn't see anything clearly for the ship had gathered momentum and had gotten too far. Patrick could have sworn it looked like Fatima and she had come to see him leave. At least, that's what he wanted to believe, but he tried to focus on watching for the tiniest of detail to make sure it was her, but it was of no use. All he could do for now was promise himself that he would do what it takes to return and meet her again soon.

Chapter 9
Mutual Jealousy

Fatima watched the ship become a tiny fleck until it disappeared. She was confident that Patrick was going to return soon, but it would be a long wait for her. Climbing down from the cliff, she couldn't help fantasizing all the fancies and dreams that a girl, in love, imagines. She kept replaying the scenes, wondering about when she was in Patrick's arms, dancing with the man of her dreams. She had never believed in love at first sight. She thought this was only possible in fiction, and yet here she was, in love with a man that she had met a few hours ago.

In her heart, she wanted to believe that Patrick had also seen her standing at the cliff, and he too longed for her. She was in a state of euphoria, utterly oblivious to everything around her. She was beaming brightly, glowing, and lilting her way down the foot of the hill. On the other hand, Sabah, too, stood at the docks, watching Brian's ship sail away. She regretted she didn't get the chance to spend time with him. She loved Brian so much that she felt her heart was going to explode.

Love-struck, Sabah would play out scenarios in which the ship was sailing peacefully on the sea and had only two passengers on board, Brian and herself. She would imagine what it would be like if the two were alone on the ship without a care for the world. Sabah was daydreaming about Brian, and it brought a daze over her. She returned to reality and looked around to see if anyone was watching her standing alone and aimlessly at this hour. She looked towards the other side of the docks to find none other than Fatima, making her way down from the cliff. It was so surprising to see Fatima there.

Fatima was smiling to herself; she looked so happy that there was a prominent glow on her face. Sabah needed to stare at Fatima, but for one moment, to be certain in the next. Fatima was in love. Only a woman in love has that look swooning on her face, and Sabah recognized it, curious as to who she was in love with. She thought that it was strange that Fatima was coming down at the exact same time Brian's ship had left. It became clear to her. It was someone from Brian's ship. That was the only logical explanation. Sabah was confused. Fatima wasn't the kind of girl to fall in love with a man quickly and easily. She hadn't seen Fatima talk to another man after her husband's death. Fatima never accepted the advances of any man ever since that incident, so all of this was shocking to Sabah. She wanted to know who it was. Her mind was imagining various scenarios at that time. She began thinking about the festival night. She had seen her father, Ahmed, had introduced Brian and Patrick to everybody at the festival as he had with Fatima and Hanane. She also recalled that Brian was the only one who had made an effort to talk to Fatima and Hanane. Patrick, on the other hand, was too occupied talking to other people at the table.

It was then that Sabah realized that the only two men who were invited from the ship were Patrick and Brian, and since Brian had conversed with her cousins, she concluded that Fatima had fallen for Brian. The suspicion immediately stung her. She wasn't going to let anyone take Brian away from her – ever. Her fists immediately coiled at the thought of losing Brian to someone else. In truth, Sabah had left her table a couple of minutes before the dance began to meet some of her friends. She hadn't returned as the dance played on, which meant that she had also not seen that Ahmed had asked Fatima and Hanane to go on the dance floor to enjoy themselves. Sabah hadn't seen the dance where the partners kept changing. She was oblivious to the moment where Fatima had become Patrick's dance partner, and how they both had gotten lost in each other's eyes only to fall in love with each other. Due to this lack of knowledge, Sabah continued believing that it was Brian with whom Fatima had fallen in love with. She snapped out of her thoughts as Fatima spotted and waved at her from the foot of the hill. She was calling for Sabah, who was making her way to Fatima anyway. Both smiled at each other in a feigned manner, and both had different reasons to do so.

Fatima didn't want Sabah to know that she was infatuated with Patrick and had gone up the hill to watch him sail away. Sabah, on the other hand, simply didn't want Fatima to steal her man from her. The two girls greeted each other like they normally do and were walking back to Sabah's home together. Both walked quietly, side by side, thinking about why they were both present at the docks. The awkwardness between the two was very evident to each. They both were trying to figure out a way to start a conversation without sounding too curious or angry.

"It is such a beautiful view from up there. If I lived here, I would watch the sunrise every morning. What about you, Sabah? Do you go and stand at the docks often this early in the morning?" Fatima broke the silence.

Sabah looked at her with a mixture of jealousy and anger. She tried to cover all of that with a smile.

"I don't come here every day. But today was an exception. Today was an extraordinary day," Sabah did her best to sound normal.

It was Fatima's turn to speak without having a trace of bitterness or jealousy in her tone.

"That is a beautiful coincidence. It was a special morning for me, too, like no other." She wanted to stop with that, but then she added, *"It becomes special when every beat of your heart starts strumming the name of a man, and you know that his heart beats for you too."*

Fatima was now prancing more than walking. She wanted to show Sabah how happy she was. Fatima would hum a melody every now and then while scampering. Sabah's anger and frustration were building up with every passing second.

She felt as if Fatima was trying to tease her with her ways just to get a reaction from her. Sabah wanted to stay indifferent and not show any interest in Fatima's story. Still, she couldn't control herself any longer, and she burst out, saying, *"Well then do tell who this mystery man of yours is? How did both of you meet?"* Sabah tried to look like her normal self while clutching the hem of her dress in anger.

Fatima looked at her with a smile then said, *"We met yesterday during the festival. We were on the dance floor. That's where we met. It looked like he didn't know how to dance because he was trying to match his steps with mine. It was adorable. Then both our hands intertwined by chance, and suddenly everything was a blur around us. It was a moment where we both did nothing except stare into each other's eyes. Oh, Sabah, if I could, I would live that moment over and over again."*

Sabah couldn't contain her anger anymore. Sabah recalled that she had come back after meeting her friends eventually only to see that everyone was on the dance floor. There were so many people there, and all of them helped Brian and Patrick dance to the music. Fatima happened to be one of the people who helped the foreigners. She had seen Fatima come on the dance floor on her father's insistence and had agreed to show the boys how to dance. She had joined Brian first and had shown him a few moves only to move to Patrick later. Sabah was shaking with anger. Her jealousy and anger blinded her so much that she couldn't even think for a second about the possibility that the person with whom Fatima had fallen in love with could have been Patrick. Sabah paced faster to the point she was almost sprinting, leaving Fatima behind.

She tried to let it go, to not think of it so much, to comfort herself that Brian's devotion was for her, but she couldn't hold it inside her any longer. She turned around and yelled, *"Who do you think you are coming here and meddling with other people's lives? Do you think you can come and steal Brian away from me? Let me tell you that Brian loves me, and I love him, ever since the day we met each other for the first time. I can't believe you would turn out exactly like your sister, who only thinks about herself. I can't believe you would think even about snatching him away from me. Brian is mine; do you understand?"* Sabah concluded and let out a sigh of relief.

Fatima stared at her cousin, extremely shocked, then burst into a fit of laughter. She couldn't control herself. This angered Sabah even further. She thought Fatima was making fun of her. Sabah leaped towards Fatima, stood right in front of her, and extended her arm making Fatima believe she might slap her.

Sabah shouted, *"You think this is all a joke? You think I am joking?"*

Fatima's next reaction was rather unexpected for Sabah. She pulled her in a hug and began kissing her forehead. Sabah tried to push her away, but it didn't work.

"What are you doing? Let go of me." Sabah squealed and squirmed, still seeing red.

Fatima stilled her and looked in her eyes and said, *"Patrick."*

Sabah still struggled to move away; she couldn't hear what Fatima had said, but it didn't sound like Brian.

"What did you say?" Sabah asked.

"Patrick, Sabah, Patrick. I was talking about Patrick all along." Fatima repeated herself with a look of glee and

shyness playing on her face, while Sabah clapped her hands over her mouth in understanding.

"Oh my God, Fatima. I am so sorry. I am so stupid. I didn't think for one second that it could be Patrick. Oh my god, all those terrible things I said ... I feel awful."

Sabah held Fatima's hand as she pled to her. *"I am so sorry. I got blinded at the thought of ... Ugh. Please forgive me. I am a terrible person."*

"Don't be silly. I am equally guilty. I am sorry for the way I behaved, and also for the ambiguity. I should have been upfront. I also thought that you loved Patrick; that's why I behaved the way I did.

But it is true though. You are very mean when you are angry. But it's okay. At least this way, we both found out the truth," Fatima consoled her cousin.

They both burst out laughing and hugged each other. Everything was pleasant again. The pretty women sat down on the grass and rambled on and on about their respective loves. Sabah had been with Brian for a while, so she had gotten to know Patrick during this time. This was great for Fatima since Sabah would prove to be of great help for her to find out when she could see Patrick again.

"Both our gentlemen will be at the International Trade Festival this coming weekend. We can certainly arrange to meet them there," Sabah informed her with a wink.

Both continued to talk for a while before they realized it had gotten a little late. They got up and made their way back to Sabah's house hand in hand. All their worries and concerns were forgotten, left behind in the forest.

Chapter 10
Mixed Emotions

Patrick's ship was presently cruising along the waters of the Mediterranean Sea as it made its way back home. Everyone was busy on the ship, executing their chores, and taking care of the things they needed to do to keep the ship on course.

And then there was Patrick.

He had made an effort not to face his crew during the entire trip back to Gibraltar. He was worried about what they might see, something had changed. He hadn't been able to stop himself from thinking about Fatima. His heart, in a knot, had navigated off course while daydreaming about her. Everything else he had feelings for following that fateful encounter with Fatima disappeared. Even his love for navigating the sea. His reveries were anchored on one moment in time and he desperately needed to get back there.

Brian steered the ship on each of their journeys back home to Gibraltar so that there was a responsible replacement for himself in case something happened.

Aaahhh! He couldn't stop thinking about Fatima, her form, her grace, her delicate voice, and her gorgeous laugh. Patrick would also wonder about the possibility of a life with her, which brought mixed emotions. He thought about his nature and then hers, about her beauty and then questioned his own looks. Did they match, did they look good together, was he elegant enough, what if just being a captain wasn't enough and lastly, did she have feelings for him? In his mind, it seemed impossible.

It felt to him as if he was sailing in a storm in unknown waters. Given his many fantasies and thoughts, he experienced mood swings. He would go from happy to sad, to thoroughly annoyed, within a matter of seconds. He didn't know what was really wrong with him. He was in a whirlwind of emotions and didn't know what to make of it.

This situation was new to Patrick; he had never felt anything like this in his life. He wanted to make sense of this enchanting distraction, for he didn't understand any of it. Was this love, a lustful desire, or maybe just an emotional phase of being lonely that would fade away with time? During all this ruminating time, he wasn't able to do anything else but try to understand his confusing predicament. As the ship sailed closer to Gibraltar's banks, Brian looked up and whistled in the direction of the crow's nest. Knots popped his head out immediately. Brian and Knots had come up with their own sign language to communicate without anyone else knowing what they were talking about. Brian signalled him to ask if he could see the captain anywhere on the ship. Knots started scanning the ship and took a good look everywhere. He then stopped and pointed towards the stern of the ship, indicating that Patrick was back there. Brian nodded to thank him while tying the helm with a rope tied to a pillar and made his way towards the back of the ship.

Patrick was leaning on the ship's sturdy fence with his monocular telescope in hand. Brian approached, and Patrick had heard him come from behind but didn't move. He was sure Brian was oblivious to everything that was happening around him, and Patrick didn't feel like sharing. Patrick thought that if he ignored Brian, he would go away. Brian, on the other hand, wanted to figure out why Patrick's mood was so daunting and stuck around, even while being ignored. They both had known each other for a very long time. Two friends that have seen nearly all sides of each other. But Brian was questioning that very thought while looking at

Patrick's back. He stood there for minutes, waiting for Patrick to budge. It was disconcerting since Brian had never seen his friend behave this way. He whistled to draw Patrick's attention and caught Patrick off guard. He thought that Brian had left. This startled him, so he turned around to see if Brian was really the one standing behind him. *"Brian, it's you. I didn't hear you come around. Seemingly, I was a bit lost in my thoughts,"* Patrick said.

"Iy, sorry about that. Umm ... Listen, captain. Not to sound arrogant or anything, but don't you think it would be better if you used the monocular spyglass while standing in front of the ship? I mean, that is the direction we are headed in. Also, we will be arriving at the docks soon. We are concerned and awaiting your instructions ... captain," Brian smirked.

Patrick let out a chuckle. He just realized that he wasn't the only one who was aware that he was standing on the stern deck, clueless and lost. He looked at Brian and gathered himself. *"Yes, of course. Certainly."* He brought the device up to take a look at the front of the ship. *"I believe we are sailing in the right direction matey. You must continue on your way ahead,"* he said without looking at Brian and then excused himself to make his way to the front of the ship. Brian climbed to the upper deck and retook charge of the steer. He couldn't help but grin regarding Patrick's behavior. He continued to observe him while steering the ship because this was surprisingly, a new facet of Patrick, one he had never seen. His friend, the captain, trudged to the front of the ship and the entire crew grew wary of Patrick's changed behavior. Patrick observed everyone looking at him and tried to busy himself, but their discerning look was too obvious. Their eyes went everywhere he did. He tried not to pay attention to them, but he couldn't sustain it any longer.

"Is something wrong? Do you want to say something? Or you're just going to keep staring at me like I'm some sort of sea monster?" he asked them. None of them said anything but passed snide comments in hushed voices, which all pretty much related to the captain allegedly getting drunk or he had met someone remarkably interesting the night before. Intuitively, that felt like the only explanation to them. Even though the crew had immense respect and gratitude for their captain, the entire situation was too funny to ignore. Every member of the crew on deck roared with laughter by the time he had gotten to the front of the ship.

The crew was on the right track and extremely witty; they chose to believe that Patrick had met an interesting lady the night before, drinking wasn't much of a thing for the captain. Everyone's thought kind of sounded a bit like this...

"Our captain had gone out one night and came back without saying a word to anyone?" "He woke up the next morning with his head and actions all disoriented and continued to stay silent?" While sailing back home, they discussed all this amongst themselves and realized Patrick wasn't anything else but a heartbeat away from love.

Patrick didn't appreciate their gossips and their continuous laughter. He turned around and gave them a very stern look. The laughter and the murmurs died in an instant; they knew what that look meant. The time for fun and games was over and within a few moments, they scattered back to their duties.

Patrick couldn't shake off his sentiment of what had to be described as a sentiment of love and continued to daydream, but his crew did make him feel self-conscious of his actions on board the ship. And so, he leaned on the gallery's fence of the ship and revisited the entire scene after he had met Fatima. He realized that his actions had to appeared to be really funny to his crew. Patrick grinned, becoming fully aware it was extremely comical to see him act this way. His urge to laugh grew strong and he couldn't hold it any longer. He suddenly broke out, laughing with the loudest of cackles.

The crew raised their heads, baffled. They looked at each other in a way that meant *"The captain has definitely gone mad,"* but Patrick was laughing so hard that they couldn't help themselves from joining him, so they all started to laugh. The laughter continued till they had tears in their eyes, some of them guffawed so hard it gave them a sore tummy. Eventually, the laughter reduced itself to chuckles and finally diminished to a state of serenity. As they got back into a calm state of mind, they once again returned to their chores.

The ship docked, and the crew carefully unloaded the freight. Patrick told Brian he was going to have a word with Miguel, and he should take over the ship to oversee the cargo. Even though everyone had stopped laughing and being silly about Patrick's love-struck situation, Brian wasn't done just yet. After Patrick told him he should watch over the ship, Brian replied, using an erotic voice, *"Of course, sweetheart, I'd do anything in the world for me captain,"* then giggled. Patrick shook his head in a defeating way and left. He didn't want to add anything else to that. He had other things on his mind. There wasn't really anything important he wanted to discuss with Miguel. He just wanted to find out if there were any deliveries to be carried out to Tangier before the International Trade Show event next weekend.

He also wanted to make sure that he was the one to carry out these deliveries. He knocked on Miguel's office door and entered upon hearing, *"Come in."* Without giving any time to Miguel to greet him, Patrick asked Miguel about any deliveries going to Tangier. Miguel frowned and turned in his chair, picking up his delivery charts to see if he had any shipments to Tangier.

Miguel was delighted to hear his captain ask about Tangier because, coincidentally, the routine delivery to Tangier had been postponed due to the International Trade Show. Patrick heard Miguel's reply and grew a bit bitter. *"Great! That's just perfect,"* he said. *"When you want something to happen it mostly never does, but the adversities just run after you with no restrictions at all... Life, huh!"* Patrick murmured to himself.

Patrick stomped his foot onto the wooden floor and walked out of Miguel's office. Instead of walking back towards the ship, he quickly turned towards the stables, got onto his horse, and galloped on his way home. Miguel was startled and confused, he had gotten up to call Patrick back in, but by the time he reached the door, Patrick had disappeared. Moments later, as Miguel was walking back to his office desk, he heard a horse riding by. This time, he quickly turned around and rushed out the door to see Patrick riding away on his horse. *"What in God's name just happened?"* Miguel exclaimed as he made his way to the ship to see Brian.

Patrick's mind was in a blur; his heart was in pain as well, and his stomach was in a knot, aching most unpleasantly. He was aware that he couldn't possibly be of any use to anyone in this condition. For these reasons, he didn't feel like getting back to the ship and made his way home. Along the way, his thoughts were nothing else but Fatima. He repeatedly tried to think about something else, literally anything that could or would take his mind off her. He tried thinking about his mother, his ship, Brian, just anything, but nothing seemed to work. He felt helpless.

It was as if he had lost control of his own mind. He arrived home and felt a bit relieved. Home was definitely the place to be. He composed himself and took a deep breath before opening the door and stepping inside the house. He went from one room to the other looking for his mother, just like he did every time he walked into the house. Catherine was in the kitchen doing the dishes, humming a tune. Being so concentrated on her dishes, she didn't hear Patrick come in. Patrick gave her a peck on the cheek and greeted her.

Hello mother," he said vivaciously and flashed a big smile at her.

She jumped a little where she was standing. *"My God, you gave me a scare. I wasn't expecting you."*

Patrick pranced across the kitchen, grabbed an apple from the basket that was kept in the middle of the table, pulled out a chair, and sat facing the back of the chair towards his mother. Catherine was surprised by the sudden change in her otherwise shy, introverted son who refrained from showing any emotions whatsoever. She continued with her chore when she suddenly stopped, dried her hands, and turned around to look at Patrick. *"Thank you for that son,"* while touching her cheek. *"You haven't done that in a long while.*

Now let me ask you this, did something happen? Did lightning strike your ship? Is everything okay?" she snickered. *"Come on, mom. It's nothing like that. Nothing happened,"* he said with a muffled voice chewing a big bite of his apple. He got up from his chair and went ahead to help her with the dishes. He began washing the dishes, lathering every pot, every utensil with bubbly foam. Catherine continued to stare at Patrick in amazement. He had never behaved this way or voluntarily helped her in any of the house chores unless he was asked to do so. This was really baffling for her. She didn't know what to make of this change in his behavior.

"Good heavens, Patrick," she said. *"I know something has indeed hit you over the head if not lightning. But whatever it is, the results are outstanding. By all means, keep getting hit by it more often,"* she said as they both ruptured into laughter. Patrick was amused by his mother's humor. Catherine, on the other hand, wasn't entirely sold by his behavior. She knew there was a reason behind all this generosity, which was most definitely new and unexplainable.

Catherine went back to washing the dishes while Patrick dried them with a cloth. She was still trying to figure out what the matter was. She restrained herself from asking him the same question again until her curiosity got the better of her.

"Okay, that's it. Give me that," she snapped, taking away the cloth from his hand. *"You don't really want to help me do the dishes; I know that much. Go and sit down at the table and wait for me,"* gesturing him towards the kitchen's dining table. *"I have made some banana bread for you; I'll cut you a few fresh slices and pour you a glass of milk. Just sit down, I'll bring it out to you, and we can talk about what is going on,"* she said with a confused but sly smile. Catherine was a mother after all, and she had her suspicions about what was going on. She just wasn't sure.

Patrick nodded with a meek smile obediently. She was right. He really didn't want to do the dishes. It was just an excuse to draw his mother's attention. He had all these feelings and emotions going around in his head, and he really didn't know what to make of them. He just wanted to talk to someone he could trust, someone mature before he would go insane. And who better than his own mother to talk about this huge delicate secret of his. He knew he could trust her with his painful condition, and she would most probably give him the best advice without turning it into a joke.

Patrick daydreamed on as he waited for his mother at the table. Ten minutes later, she walked towards him, carrying a heavily laden tray. She placed it on the table, dried off her hands on her apron, and sat down on the chair next to Patrick. The banana bread with the serving of homemade jam and buttermilk looked heavenly delicious. She pushed the tray closer to Patrick to entice him and said, *"Okay, son. Start talking. I know something is bothering you, so let's just get right to it. Tell me."*

Patrick had never felt so shy and uncomfortable in front of his mother before. He didn't know where to begin and how to put this into words. He didn't know exactly how to bare his heart out to her about a situation like the one he was caught in. He wondered a lot about how he would be able to explain this, and so he decided to take a little detour. He began questioning his mom about his father, knowing very well that this might be quite similar to his situation, and would be much easier to about openly.

He began by saying, *"Tell me, mother, how did you know dad was the right one for you? The ... you know ... How did you know... How did you know he was your soul mate?"* Catherine was a little taken aback. She wasn't expecting Patrick to pose that question. Even though she knew sooner or later Patrick would ask about his father, this particular timing came as a surprise. But Catherine had the answer ready. She had stopped thinking about it when she saw Patrick wasn't exactly interested in discussing the topic. But on this day, finally, she was glad that he had brought it up.

Catherine inhaled and exhaled slowly. She was careful in selecting her words and began. *"Hmmm ... I'm glad you brought this up, this is sincerely the easiest question to answer out of all the questions you could have asked me. It was quite an easy decision for me. I knew he was the right one because my heart guided me to him, and through the entire relationship we had, no matter how short-lasting, I fell in love with him, even more, each day. I was listening to what my heart was telling me. If I had gone against this, that would have meant being dishonest with myself,"* she breathed slowly again and then continued.

"When we met for the first time, he was injured. But even so, my heart started racing for him at the touch of his hand, and with every heartbeat came a powerful sensation of inner joy. He soon became the focal point of my life, the center of my world. He is not with us today, God Bless his soul, but he continues to be a part of me and will always be the center of my world. Today, only in my heart, will he have the opportunity to live as long as I do." She had grown emotional and finished her sentence as she wiped her eyes.

At that moment, much to Catherine's surprise, mother's intuition came alive, and Catherine's earlier suspicions of what might be tormenting Patrick's mind tingled again. She felt what was encapsulating his mind and his thoughts. *So, this is really happening,* she thought to herself. *Well, glory is to God; he has met a girl and has finally fallen in love.* She didn't mention anything but spoke again, *"Now it's time for me to give you the answer to your real question."*

Patrick realized that his mom caught on to his feelings of love and attempted to open his mouth to deny anything of the sort, but Catherine raised a finger to her lips to ensure that it was okay. She was well aware of what he was going through. He didn't need to be shy or secretive about it. She was his mother, and if he were going to discuss any of this to anyone, it would be best for it to be her. Catherine continued to explain certain particulars of love, being one of the most complex, complicated, and unnerving mysteries of life. She told him that the earliest poems in the world started with being about love. She explained that poets keep on trying to capture it, but it's impossible to crack the enigma. She talked of laborious journeys lovers took, the abnegation, the trials in kings' courts. *"It's usually after many perils that lovers obtain the person they desire. I sure was lucky in your father's case, though."*

Everything she said made sense, but it wasn't enough in order to give him the patience and will to bear the trials. All he could do now was to brace himself until time past getting him to the day of the International Trade Show that was supposed to take place next week. Which, in fact, wasn't too far away.

He hoped that Fatima would be there. *"She had to be,"* he thought. He even thought about pulling some strings to ensure she'd be there just to meet with him again. Since Brian's girlfriend, Sabah happened to be her cousin. It might be worth asking her if she knew if Fatima would be there next weekend. He didn't quite know how he was going to make this work though. But suddenly, while thinking about next weekend, he felt crushed just thinking he had to wait a whole week before seeing her again. And that was true only if she had plans to be at the Trade Show.

"s i g h!" Patrick sighed in anguish.

Chapter 11
A Second Chance

The long-awaited day of the International Trade Festival was finally here. This festival took place every year at the docks of Tangier. It was one of the most important, and most looked forward events in the city. Traders traveled to Tangier from across the globe to participate in this trade show.

It had begun as a small trade event that was only limited to Tangier and some other cities in Morocco. Since the first event was such a big success, it became an annual function and people came from everywhere. Ships filled with travelers and trade goods would sail into the port of Tangier just to be a part of this event.

It was an opportunity for international traders and merchants to exhibit their products and goods to the people of Morocco, as well as to international travelers. Amongst the many ships docked in the port, Patrick's ship was one of them. Like every year, he stocked a great deal of variety of trade goods from England. Other ships were carrying goods that came from countries far and wide, presenting a spectacle of foreign cultures as the displays were laid out. The trade show was a perfect place for the people of Morocco, as well as foreign visitors from all over the world, to see the latest innovations, inventions, recipes, clothing, and everything new to the world. Also, if one happened to have the money to purchase the products on display, they could do that too.

This event had gained widespread popularity in the Middle East. The ports of Morocco gleamed with diverse beauty and cultures coming from people everywhere around the globe. The traders, merchants, and visitors alike would arrive days in advance not to miss out on the festivities the trade show had to offer.

Patrick's ship was anchored near the central area of the port. This area was one of the busiest for trade on the docks. As Patrick was stepping off the ship, he had assigned Knots to supervise the trade goods stored in and on the ship. The little man also had to make sure that their trade goods were ready to be displayed. Making his way off the ship, Patrick could not stop himself from admiring the German ship docked next to his. It was a massive vessel built with the latest state of the art crafts.

Patrick was immediately attracted to its design and build and could definitely imagine himself sailing this ship across the ocean. His curiosity, urging him to see more of the ship, overwhelmed him with a desire to admire its artistry and craftsmanship. So, Patrick stepped on board the German ship to take a closer look.

The captain of the ship was present in his quarters and saw Patrick walk on deck. Out of curiosity, he walked out of his quarters to greet the stranger. Patrick introduced himself and shook hands with the gentleman. The German captain also introduced himself in English using a strong German accent and called himself Karl. He soon learned that Patrick was also a captain, and their ships were anchored next to each other.

Karl also noticed Patrick's interest in his ship and began telling him some fascinating facts about the ship. While they were talking, more people had walked onboard the ship. By the time the captain was done telling Patrick about some fun facts about the ship, the main deck was bustling with people. The captain excused himself so that he could welcome and greet the others, and Patrick encouraged him. Before he left, he suggested that Patrick spare some time and study the art collection that was on display inside. Patrick nodded as the German captain attended other guests and entered the quarters. Everything was made and curated in Germany. Patrick's eyes widened with each frame and work of art he laid eyes on. He figured he might just as well pick something up for his mother since she was an avid admirer of art and artistry. He decided to look at the collection more carefully so that he could choose from one of the pieces. He was still scanning the room when his eyes fell upon a clock. He immediately knew it was not an ordinary clock. It was one of those that have a wooden house built on the top, and a bird would pop out of it when the clock struck the hour.

The clock had a very exotic feel to it. The very intricately carved house, the very interestingly designed clock face, it all piqued his excitement. Patrick loved it instantly and knew his mother would love it too. He proclaimed to the clerk standing in the room who guided the onlookers about the price of the clocks. The price quoted was remarkably high, higher than Patrick had expected. He put forward a counter price, but the clerk was very difficult about it. They continued to negotiate back and forth, but the clerk had to move away for a few minutes to tend to another customer.

Patrick, feeling defeated, shifted from his spot, and walked towards the other corner of the room when he chanced upon something else that was way better than a clock. Not something but rather someone. He could clearly see a lady-like figure walking the docks of Tangier from the window. A lady-like figure that he was certain he knew. His heart began palpitating instantly. Without a doubt, Patrick was confident that he was looking at the love of his life, who was surprisingly in Tangier for the Trade Show.

His heartbeat surged with every step she took. Taking in her every movement, he filled himself with the delicacy she was. Patrick had waited the entire week for this to happen without knowing that Fatima would be here, but there she was. Suddenly his heart almost suffered a stroke when the clerk's arrival obstructed his view from the window. He had returned to show him a different but similar clock.

Patrick had forgotten about the clock. His attention had been redirected to someone far more interesting and his interest in the clock had faded away. He vaguely shook his head showing the clerk that he was not interested in purchasing the clock. The clerk replied, but Patrick was not paying attention and desperately trying to look outside over the clerk's shoulder. Following Patrick's reaction, the clerk sat down to retrieve another item beneath the lower shelf, thinking that Patrick might be interested in something else. The moment the clerk stepped aside and cleared Patrick's line of sight, she became visible again, and his heart resumed with excitement. He could watch her take each step carefully across the dock while imagining himself holding her hand, helping her get through the obstacles.

Patrick swiftly pulled himself out of his state of hypnosis after having that thought and quickly walked out of the room in view of getting off the ship. The clerk, watching Patrick walk by, stood up, holding a smaller version of the clock that had caught Patrick's interest. Since it was paper-wrapped, Patrick did not see the clock while passing by and really wasn't bothered with what the clerk was holding.

The clerk had figured it would have fallen into Patrick's price range, but he only saw Patrick leave in a hurry. How rude, the clerk exclaimed to himself. He shrugged his shoulders, put the clock back in its place, and busied himself with other customers, many of whom had picked up items of their choice and were also ready to barter with the clerk. Patrick got off the German ship as fast as he could. He wanted to catch up with Fatima without wasting any more time looking at the German art collection, but there was a sea of people out there. All you could see was bobbing heads entering the city through the docks. The festival's turnout increased with every passing year, and it was extremely challenging to spot someone in the crowd from a distance. Mostly anyone else would have lost sight of Fatima the very same moment they had spotted her, but not Patrick. Even among all the people, he had his eyes fixed on her, and he made sure that he did not lose sight of her.

He noticed that she was walking towards his ship and that she had stepped onto the ramp to board it. Patrick, not having any thought about what he would say to her once he caught up, was not so far behind. Every step he took became an eager one to get closer to the woman he loved, and as he trimmed his way through the crowd, he became anxious. Seconds away from his ship, Patrick could almost smell the scent of her skin. Finally, an opening in the crowd paved a pathway for Patrick to his ship, but in his haste to take a turn, he misjudged his steps and collided into a slave. The slave was carrying one side of a crate while another slave was carrying the other.

All three men fell onto the dock with a din. Patrick's sudden impact made the cargo fly in mid-air, which fell with a deafening crash. The noise and the commotion attracted attention from a lot of people, especially those near the incident. Many people stopped in their ways to see what was going on. Some people came forward to help them while others stopped for a second, then continued with their matters.

Fatima, being awfully close, jumped the minute she heard the deafening crash as she was taking her last step off the ramp onto Patrick's ship. She had already been extremely nervous about being on the ship to meet Patrick, and then the loud noise practically spooked her out. With her hand on her chest, after being able to calm herself down, Fatima stopped and turned around to see what was going on.

She spotted people gathered at a particular area on the dock near Patrick's ship, and that was all she could see. Patrick was not in her line of sight, and she could not understand the chaos because of all the people surrounding the incident. In his fall, Patrick hit his head against the wooden cargo crate, and as a result, he had passed out the moment he hit the ground. Many people had gathered around to help him regain consciousness. Fatima only ended up seeing a swarm of concerned people while being unaware that the man she loved, whom she had been dreaming about for a whole week, was lying unconscious beneath the crowd. Due to this lack of awareness, Fatima was not much interested in the incident on the dock. She turned around and made her way towards the items being sold on Patrick's ship, hoping to get a glimpse of the man she holds dear in her heart.

While looking at the items, Fatima could not avoid noticing that a little man was following her every movement. This little man was indeed Knots keeping an eye on the merchandise. She would turn away from an item to study another, and he would follow her with the exact amount of footsteps. Fatima decided to play along and smiled while being amused at how accurate Knots could be in his movements. In a flash, she quickly turned around and slightly bent her knees to see eye to eye with the little man, asking him, "*Are you following me, little man?*" Knots' eyes widened with surprise as he answered with a smile, nodding his head up and down and repeatedly pulling the bandana he tied around his neck.

"*You are!*" Fatima answered with a smile, and Knots nodded again in the same way. Fatima replied, *"Well, maybe you can help me."* Knots nodded again in the same way, thinking to himself that she was such a beautiful lady. He wanted to help her with anything she wanted.

Fatima continued, *"Okay then, can you tell me who the captain of the ship is?"* Knots was still nodding in the same way, but he tapped on his chest, illustrating that he was the ship's captain. Fatima replied sarcastically to his gesture, *"Really, then your name must be Patrick. Am I right?"* Knots holds his chin while tapping his foot and frowned, thinking, *maybe you're not all that nice after all.* He quickly shook his head from side to side. Fatima giggled, saying, *"You might not be the captain, but you certainly have the heart to be one someday."*

Knots took a bit of time to figure out what was said and then said to himself, okay, she's beautiful again and smiled while showing Fatima an index finger, asking her to wait for a moment. Knots then rushed into the captain's quarters, and of course, Fatima thought he was going to inform Patrick of her presence. All her nervousness returned, and she started fiddling with the locks of her hair absentmindedly. Knots rushed out of the captain's quarters wearing a captain's hat and held a pink carnation in his hands. While showing the captain's hat to Fatima, he pointed towards the off-ramp showing Fatima that Patrick had left. Fatima confirmed with a question, *"Patrick has left the ship?"* Knots agreed and took her hand to offer her the pink carnation.

Fatima was grateful for the offering, a pink carnation meant gratitude and never to be forgotten. As warm-hearted as she was, she kissed Knots on the forehead and thanked him for being such a sweetheart. She then made her way to the off-ramp and walked down the ramp onto the docks. She walked past the group of people who were still gathered because of Patrick's incident. Fatima glanced a bit but didn't insist and kept walking ahead.

She was so engrossed in her thoughts that she didn't even suspect that Patrick could be the reason for the crowd, if not amidst the group. Back at the incident, a concerned citizen was getting ready to splash a bucket of cold water on Patrick's face. Upon receiving all that water, Patrick heaved, opened his eyes, and sat up, coughing out the water that had entered his mouth. He rubbed his eyes dry to take a good look at what was happening around him.

The first thing Patrick saw when his vision cleared was the black man he had collided with, who was as big as an ox. For a minute, Patrick thought he had woken up in the land of the giants.

His mind cleared almost immediately, and Fatima's thoughts ran through his head, making him remember how he got into this mess in the first place. Patrick jolted upright and dusted off his wet clothing. Taking a good look around, Fatima was nowhere to be seen. He reckoned she might still be on the ship.

Squirming past the crowd muttering *"Excuse me"* and *"Sorry,"* he finally spotted his on-ramp, ran towards it, leaped onto it, and ran onto the ship as fast as possible.

As soon as Patrick got on board, he began looking for Fatima. She was nowhere to be found. While making his way back to the off-ramp, he stopped in his tracks and noticed Knots standing there with his mouth gaped, smiling with one of the most annoying smiles.

Knots ran his eyes on Patrick and tried to read the expression on his face, then said, *"Hey, boss? You back early. You looking for someone?"* Patrick knew at that moment that Knots was aware of whom he had come looking for but still tried to feign ignorance. *"No, no. Why would you ask of that?"* Patrick said abruptly. Knots raised his eyebrow. *"Huh ... well then. I was about to tell you words, words she told me, you know, beautiful lady words!"* said with a grin on his face, *"But, I don't think these words are good to you. Hmmm? How do you say? Yes ... Yes, these words no important to you. So ... I am just going to go now. See you later,"* Knots replied in his own broken language, shrugging as he decided to walk away.

"Hey, KNOTS!" Patrick yelled, and that was when Knots made a run for it. He began running around the ship, and Patrick made several attempts to catch him, but the little man was just too fast. Knots put his full agility to work, running from one place to another like a frantic little monkey but Patrick wasn't surprised by Knots' agility and knew that he would be hard to catch.

This event caught the entire crew's attention as they watched Patrick and Knots chase each other like a game of cat and mouse. They weren't aware of the reason why this was happening but enjoyed the scene, nonetheless. Knots leaped forward onto the shroud and headed for the poop deck at the back of the ship. He made sure there was no way Patrick could easily catch him. The captain was out of breath; he had not run that much in a long while. He stopped and slouched down to grab onto his knees to catch his breath. Knots laughed as he saw Patrick panting as if he had just run a 10-mile marathon. Once his breath had begun to even up, he looked at Knots and yelled, *"Okay, Knots. You got me. You're too fast for me."* he began. Knots smirked.

Patrick continued, *"Let's make a deal. You tell me what I want to know, and you can dine in the captain's cabin tonight. You'll have all the food and drinks you desire. Does that sound good?"* he presented his offer. Knots was compelled to consider the proposition. He knew that was an offer only a fool would refuse.

He also knew the food served to the captain was a lot better than anything he had ever eaten. He accepted the offer, Patrick walked close to the shroud where Knots was hanging, and they both shook hands. He then recounted the complete story of how his lady love had come on board the ship looking for him. *"She asked about you and was a little disappointed when I told her that you had left the ship,"* he finished. Knots did not think it was appropriate to tell Patrick about the flower. He didn't want to give Patrick an excuse to take away his feast. Patrick sighed and passed a hand over his still wet head. He really wanted to see Fatima, and he shook his regret away. *"Knots, quickly tell me in which direction she turned when she left the ship?"* Patrick asked. Knots gestured towards the far-right side of the ship. Patrick, without losing any time, thanked Knots and moved towards the front of the ship.

Knots came down the shroud and bellowed after him, *"Hey, Cap. Nothing personal, eh! I was just playing with you."* Patrick turned and smiled at him, *"C'mon little man, It's nothing, no harm done. As promised, tonight you dine with me and tomorrow, you scrub the decks. Good deal, eh?"* he said and left. Patrick's reply did not amuse Knots. He was trying to figure out if Patrick was joking or if he actually meant it.

Patrick was jogging past the docks in Fatima's direction, and he could not believe how many people had arrived for the trade event. The port was flooded in every direction. Patrick felt as if a quarter of the world's population had landed in Tangier. He was equally surprised by how big the trade event had become and how many people had come to be a part of it. Patrick loved the Trade Show and everything about it. However, it was the first time that he hated the crowd. It would require a magician to find Fatima amidst all these people. She could be anywhere, and he didn't have a clue where to begin the search, but he did hope that he would eventually find her if he kept looking. An hour passed, and his hopes and spirits were at an all-time low. He had finally given up on the idea of finding Fatima. *She must have left by now*, he thought to himself.

Patrick had been walking and running around without stopping for a single minute, and he had gotten exhausted. The afternoon sun was advancing towards the evening, and he was bored by the beauty of it all. He wanted to rest and sit down for a few minutes before resuming his search. Not far in front of him were a couple of stacked cargo crates settled on the docks. *"That would be the perfect place to sit and rest,"* he thought. He squeezed quickly past a couple of folks in case anyone else had the same idea.

Atop a few crates, he sat down, stretched his legs a little and a moan of relief instantly left his mouth. Tired he was, and a little heartbroken about his current situation. But nevertheless, this did not stop him from looking at all the people moving around him, especially the couples holding hands, imagining himself in that same position. Patrick turned and looked at the ships lined up at the docks and saw other people who were still getting off their ships, helping their loved ones down the ramp. He again imagined himself carrying his loved one safely down the off-ramp. If only Fatima was in the crowd he was looking at, he could have been with her. A heavy and extended sigh accompanied his thoughts.

But little did he know, Fatima was also thinking about him in a very similar way. In fact, she was daydreaming about Patrick just next to him, on the other side of the same group of crates Patrick was sitting on. If he had sat a few more feet to the left of the crates, or if Fatima had walked passed the crates, they would have seen one another. The crates were stacked in a way that they both were able to sit down on each side of them but were unable to see each other.

Fatima grew anxious and was tired of sitting down, so she pushed herself up from the crate and looked around while asking herself, *"Where to now, where would I find you in this maze of people?"* She took a few steps back, clearing the stacked crates. Turned around and searched within the crowd. Not knowing the docks very well, Fatima wasn't sure if she had looked in this area, she was a bit confused. Fatima took a few more steps back, the crates were now hiding her, but she leaned on the top crates while pulling herself up to see a greater distance.

Patrick, still sitting down, heard a thump from the crates. Distracted, he turned around but thought nothing of it and went back to his thoughts. Fatima now turned to the left side, leaned her back on the stacked crates, and got ready to choose a direction to resume the search. Patrick heard another thump coming from the crates behind him, but he wasn't going to be distracted a second time.

Had he turned around on his right side; he would have recognized the sleeve from Fatima's dress which was in plain sight. They were so close that they could have held each other's hand had they extended their arms back. But fate had other plans, Fatima was getting ready to venture completely in the opposite direction.

While searching the crowd and standing on the tip of her toes for a more unobstructed view, her eyes suddenly stopped moving. Fatima had set her eyes upon someone who looked like it could be Patrick.

Without losing an instant, she pushed herself away from the stacked crates and made her way towards this man. Patrick, still within his thoughts, wanted to stand on top of the crates and yell her name at the top of his lungs, but that would have been incredibly embarrassing, especially if there were people in the crowd who knew him. He was too bashful to carry out a feat so bold.

Patrick then said to himself, *"Enough of this, maybe she went back to the ship, or maybe not. But regardless, I do have to return to my ship."* The captain in love made his way back to the ship and learned that Fatima had not returned. Disappointed indeed, he was, but a thought glimmered like hope. He figured there could only be one reason for her to board his ship, and ask Knots about him. And that was reason enough for him and look forward to meeting her another time soon.

Chapter 12
A Third Chance

Patrick was frustrated with how things turned out as opposed to how he had imagined they would go. He was still cursing himself for not shouting out Fatima's name when he had seen her the first time. Patrick should've known that it would be impossible to find her amidst all the crowd. Disappointed and disheveled, he returned to the ship.

The crewmembers were busy carrying out their tasks when they saw the captain walk on to the ship. They all looked at him while he made his way to his cabin from the front deck, and he could feel their eyes on the back of his shoulder. There were clear signs of annoyance in his form.

He stopped in his tracks and turned around to face them. *"Listen to me very carefully. I want to see Brian immediately. If you see him, send him to me, and this goes for everyone. The first one to see him, tell him to come and see me. I will be in my quarters,"* he ordered in a very stern tone.

"Yes, captain." All of them nodded their heads.

Patrick didn't wait for the crew to say anything else. He was done talking. He strode to his quarters, taking giant leaps at a time. He pushed the door open and barged in, anger and frustration stamped across his face. He hated the feeling of being so helpless, and as he passed by the spit bowl, he kicked it out of his way with such force that it went flying across the room and landed with a deafening sound.

He pulled out the chair and sat down at the table, banging it with his fist.

"Why did everything have to happen this way? Why?" speaking out loud in the room. There was no one in his quarters, yet he was waiting for someone to answer.

Realizing that no one would answer, he continued, more despondent this time, *"We were so close; I could feel her presence around me in that crowd. Why did it have to happen this way?"* He began diving deeper into his own thoughts.

Patrick had been waiting for the festival for a whole week, which had seemed like a lifetime. And he was not even sure if she would show up at the event. He was counting down hours and minutes before he could see Fatima again, and today he had that chance. He was so close, but it seemed like it was far away, entirely out of his reach. All the wait and anticipation had been for nothing. He thumped the table again in defeat.

Brian had arrived and was standing outside his cabin. He had walked onto the ship a couple of minutes ago when one of the crewmen had told him that Patrick wanted to see him immediately. Brian was feeling a little cautious because of how the message had been delivered to him, which was also backed up by the gaze of several crew members. Brian didn't know how serious this was, and he walked towards Patrick's quarters, deciding to ignore their suspicion.

As Brian walked in, he could see Patrick's vexation from over the double swing doors. Brian was petrified at that moment. He thought he had been caught judging by the look of despair and annoyance on Patrick's face. Brian presumed he had somehow found out about the stolen merchandise unaccounted for on the ship. Brian also felt that he should come clean on his own before Patrick challenged him with facts he could not deny.

He gulped down the lump in his throat and rapped on the door twice.

"Who is it?" Patrick barked. Then he lifted his head and said, *"Brian if it's you, come in. Anybody else, stay out. I don't want to see anyone else at the moment."*

Wow, Brian thought. Patrick is really in a terrible mood. He walked in and was suddenly greeted with a mist of anger and tension in the room. *"Take a seat, Brian,"* he said, bowing his head and not looking at his friend.

Brian did as he was told and sat on the chair across him. He could see Patrick's face and sensed that this wasn't going to go very well.

Patrick held his face up and looked at Brian. Brian passed him a half-smile. Patrick's face was blank. He rose up from his chair and sat on the chair next to Brian.

He looked at him intently for a moment and then said, *"Brian, I am at a point right now where I desperately need your help, and for you to help me, I want to make a confession."*

Brian felt at ease upon hearing these words. He wasn't expecting Patrick to say something like that. In fact, the scenario had taken a different turn completely. Patrick began talking and told Brian everything about Fatima and how he had fallen in love with her after seeing her for the first time. Brian clearly remembered this little encounter at the festival and listened while nodding in stupefaction. He also told Brian how much he wanted to see her again. Brian was still a little taken aback by what Patrick had told him but was finally able to figure out why Patrick had been behaving uncanny lately. This was the first time Patrick had been in love, thought Brian, and he felt quite happy for him.

But Patrick wasn't able to get a grip on his emotions, at least, not in a healthy way. Patrick then told Brian that Fatima was here at the trade show, but he hesitated to contact her when the time was right. Knowing Brian was in a relationship with Sabah, Patrick wanted Brian's advice. He was certain Brian knew how this situation should play out. Brian must have gone through those motions, Patrick thought, and therefore he was comfortable in sharing all the details with him.

He even asked for Brian's help. Brian confirmed that he would help Patrick in a heartbeat, and considering Fatima was Sabah's cousin, Brian had an idea. Since Fatima was in town, she must have been staying at Sabah's house. Brian advised Patrick to calm down and to be a little patient in this matter. He told him that he would go to Ahmed's store to see if Sabah had any idea about Fatima's whereabouts. Patrick cheered and agreed to this brilliant idea. *"I knew I could trust you with this,"* he said. Brian smiled, put a hand on his captain's shoulder, and left shortly after.

Heading towards Ahmed's store, he saw Fatima and Sabah walking away from the shop. Brian changed his direction and sprinted towards Sabah. As he got closer to them, he called out Sabah's name. They both turned around and came to a halt. Brian greeted both of them while panting and asked them if they could stay here and wait for a short while. Both Fatima and Sabah looked at each other, without any clue about why they should wait and laughed out loud.

Brian turned towards Fatima and told her, *"You must stay here, Fatima. You don't want to move away from here because there is someone who's dying to see you again. He has been waiting to see you with bated breath."* He said with a hearty laugh. Fatima looked at Sabah and shrugged. While backing up, looking at both ladies with his arms stretched out in front of him, Brian repeatedly said, *"Wait, please wait. It won't take long; I'll be right back ... please,"* and then Brian turned around to make a run for the ship.

Fatima instantly realized then what Brian was talking about Patrick. Even, she was more than certain he was referring to Patrick. Suddenly her breath caught in her throat, thinking that she was about to see Patrick again.

Brian finally got back to the ship. He ran up the ramp and was panting like a dog. He stopped, took the time to catch his breath, and then rushed into the captain's quarters. *"Patrick!"* He bellowed at the top of his lungs.

"Get up and come with me. Come quick. Fatima's at Ahmed's store." The moment Patrick heard these words, he got up from his chair and ran off the ship with Brian, and they both headed for Ahmed's store.

Again, Patrick's crew was watching all this unfold before them and thought. Okay… Patrick's unusual behavior over the last couple of days, the fact that Brian was in charge of sailing the ship while the captain was busy daydreaming in his quarters, the scene before them was the crux of it all; a woman. Also watching them both run off the ship like two young kids who had just robbed something mundane was something new and unseen. They finally all looked at each other thinking that their captain and first mate might have totally lost their minds.

Little did the boys know, while Brian was informing Patrick that Fatima was at Ahmed's place, Fatima's brother, Mohammed, pulled up with a coach asking her to get in because they were in a rush to leave. Layla was exhausted, and they had to leave immediately without wasting any time. They had a long road to travel. Fatima tried her best to stretch out time, but it proved to be futile.

Her sister was getting impatiently nasty, and she had to leave. Under duress, she hurriedly wrote a note and handed it to Sabah, telling her to make sure Patrick received it. Fatima then kissed Sabah on the cheek, hugged her dearly, and said while leaving to board the coach, *"In God's will,"* Sabah smiled back at her and repeated, *"In God's will, cousin."* The caravan departed with the sun setting behind them.

Brian and Patrick finally reached Ahmed's marketplace, but it had taken them too long. They could see the coach ride away as they grabbed onto their knees to catch their breath. Sabah came towards them with a look of sympathy and handed out Fatima's note to Patrick. He unfolded the note, looked at it, and reacted with a confused smile. He then looked up at Sabah, took a small breath, and said, *"I can't read Arabic me lady."*

He handed the note back to her, *"Could you read it for me, please? I'm dying to know what's written."*

Sabah couldn't help but feel sorry for Patrick. She looked at the piece of paper and read to herself first. She blinked, then looked at Patrick and delivered Fatima's message to him. *"Patrick, we weren't meant to meet today, but another time, another day, but very soon, I should hope."* Signed *Fatima x x.*

He was downhearted and disappointed that he had missed her again, but happy to know that Fatima came for him, and was hopeful that she wanted to see him again soon.

He looked towards the road taken by the stagecoach and muttered the words under his breath, *"Bye, Fatima. Till we meet again sometime soon."*

Chapter 13
The Plan

Patrick was exhausted and overrun with the outcomes of the day. Today, all his energy had been spent in trying to meet with Fatima, and nothing had seemed to work out in his favor. Sabah saw Patrick's displeasure and how emotionally drained he looked. She knew how that felt and everything that must have preoccupied his mind during the day.

Life has its trials, but the ones closer to the heart always end up being the most challenging. One can never get used to a situation like this one. While Sabah was thinking about Patrick and Fatima, she came up with an idea that might just work for the boys as well as for herself. It would be like killing two birds with one stone for she would also get to see Brian. She asked the boys to pay attention as she hashed out the plan.

"Next weekend, we are invited to dine at Fatima's sister's country place in Tetouan. She's sending a coach for us early in the morning."

Brian rapidly interjected, *"Tetouan? How are we supposed to get to Tetouan? We don't even know where that is. And it's not like we can get into the coach without being noticed. Plus, we're not even invited?"*

Sabah replied, *"I know ... I know, Mr. Impatient, but there is a way!"*

Both Brian and Patrick looked at each other. There were signs of curiosity and confusion written across their faces. Patrick gestured Sabah to explain further.

"The coach has a storage area beneath the floor, like a double floor. It runs across the entire base of the coach, even under the seats, so there should be enough room for both of you. All you have to do is to be here early in the morning and get in without being noticed. If you need help, I'll be here to create a distraction."

Patrick was so desperate to see Fatima that he agreed right away. According to him, it was an excellent idea, but Brian wasn't too keen on spending even a few hours lying down in a coach's storage area. Sabah looked at him with the meanest of expressions and smacked him behind the head.

Brian caressed his head and immediately proclaimed that he heartedly agreed with the plan. *"So, it's settled then,"* said Sabah, clapping her hands together.

Patrick spoke this time and raised his concern, *"What are we supposed to do when we get there? I am sure you will be staying there overnight?"* Sabah nodded.

But before any of them could say anything else, she raised her hand to stop them from speaking and explained that they would have to sneak out of the coach and hide in the stables. She would then take the time to explain the whole situation to Fatima, and only then would they both come out and meet the two girls at the stables.

"Oh great, after being knocked around for several hours on the floor of a coach, we get to sleep in a stable," Brian replied, folding his hands.

Sabah slapped his shoulder.

"Okay, okay, it's a great plan," Brian said, caressing his arm this time.

Patrick agreed too, and while leaving for the ship, he looked at Sabah and confirmed, *"See you Saturday morning."*

Brian stayed behind and waited until Patrick had his back completely turned before giving a quick peck to Sabah on the cheek. She blushed as he ran to join Patrick, then they both darted back to the ship.

Brian asked Patrick, *"Are you sure we have cargo to deliver in Tangier this Saturday?"*

"Yes, Miguel just changed the delivery dates, and we should be here Friday to leave sometime on Sunday. This schedule shouldn't change for at least another two weeks," Patrick replied.

Brian said with excitement, *"All good then, all we have to do is get ready for the great journey."* Patrick chuckled and replied, *"Iy, define great."*

The day after sailing back to Gibraltar, Patrick woke up early and left for the port. Brian had slept over but was still in bed, sound asleep and Patrick decided to let him sleep and come back for him later. Patrick wanted to make sure everything was set for Friday's crossing to Tangier. He was eager to get his ship ready for that special day. Early though it was, and Miguel happened to be waiting for him. When Patrick arrived, Miguel called him into his office and explained that he had made a mistake with the delivery dates, and according to the new schedule he had, they were going back to Tangier on Wednesday the following week. Patrick was not exactly excited about this news. He certainly needed to get back to the house and talk to Brian about this matter. Another strategy to get to Tangier on Saturday morning had become a priority.

While still bunking at Patrick's house, this made things easier to discuss and come up with another plan. Even though they had much time in front of them to change their strategy, it was unsettling for Patrick just to think that he might not get a chance to be there Saturday morning. Since there was no use getting the ship ready to sail, Patrick rushed back home to share the news with Brian.

Brian was having breakfast when Patrick walked into the house. *"Good morning, sleepyhead, where's Mum,"* Patrick said. Brian lifted his left arm to say hi, and after gulping his coffee said, *"Iy, your mum is gone to the market to fetch some eggs and flour."* Patrick replied, *" Hmm, eggs would have been good just about now."* Patrick then poured himself a cup of coffee, pulled himself a chair next to Brian, and said, *"No matter, we have something to discuss."*

Every time Patrick opened a conversation like this, it made Brian a little nervous. Brian replied, *"What about?"* *"We're not sailing the ship to Tangier on Friday,"* Patrick confirmed.

There was a moment of silence and Patrick explained why their schedule changed when suddenly Patrick took a sip of coffee and spat it back into his cup. *"Holy my Christ, did you brew this coffee, mate? Holy, mother of God, this coffee will have a horse run for days."* Brian started to laugh, *"Oh c'mon, me little sailor, it's not that bad."* However, as Brian said, *"me little sailor,"* an idea to get to Tangier flashed in his mind.

He turned to Patrick and said, *"I got an idea; we'll steal one of Miguel's little boats to get across to Tangier."*

Patrick said, *"That's a great idea, but we work for him, so we don't really have to steal it. All we have to do is write Miguel a note telling him that we borrowed the boat to go fishing and we will return it as soon as we return."*

Brian replied, *"Great plan,"* to which Patrick said, *"Iy, that will work fine mate, this shouldn't be a problem."*

On Saturday morning, the boys were at the dock at 4 o'clock. The boat was ready to leave; they had prepared the boat Friday without being noticed. They both jumped into the boat and pushed it away from the dock. From this moment on, Patrick's happiness knew no limits.

They were both giggling like young boys who had accomplished something they considered was seemingly impossible. As they were sailing away from the docks, Patrick put his hand in his pocket and closed his eyes in frustration. He had forgotten to leave the note for Miguel.

It was still in his pocket. Patrick wanted to turn back, but there wasn't any time for that. The return was bound to make them late on arrival. Patrick didn't want that, but Brian had an idea. He asked Patrick for the note and put in an empty wine bottle that was on the boat.

Patrick looked at Brian, confused. *"What are you going to do with that?"* he asked.

Brian explained that this was one of Miguel's wine bottles, and if he saw it floating around the shoreline, it was almost certain he'd find a way to fish it out of the water. Patrick liked the idea. Brian flung the bottle as hard as possible so it would drop as close to shore as possible. Patrick grinned again and patted Brian's back approvingly, and they sailed to the shores of Tangier as planned. Other than that little hiccup, everything was going just fine.

The two boys arrived at the docks of Tangier safely. They docked the boat and made their way to the marketplace as quickly as possible. As they were about to reach Ahmed's store, they saw the coach stopped outside.

Patrick looked at Brian and said, *"We are right on time, mate."*

They leaned against the house not to be seen and saw the coachman step down from the coach to announce his arrival. The coachman then proceeded towards Ahmed and started discussing, but since they were standing at a distance, the boys did not have the slightest idea what was being said. The coachman walked into the store with Ahmed, and the door closed behind him.

Patrick and Brian looked at each other and said in unison, *"This is going to be easier than we think,"* and launched into a fit of silent giggles again.

They had no control over themselves; the adrenaline had completely taken them over. Taking advantage of the situation, they both ran towards the rear of the coach. Brian opened the hatch to the double floor and got in the back face down. Patrick got in the same way, and once they were in, they closed the hatch.

Patrick looked at Brian, who was still giggling, *"We haven't been reckless like this in a long time."*

Brian had a weird look on his face when Patrick said this.

Patrick asked him, *"You don't look okay, is something wrong?"*

Brian replied, *"Not at the moment, but there might be a problem soon."*

Patrick was worried. He asked again, *"Why is that?"*

Brian replied, *"I think I ate too much banana bread this morning, and now I'm getting these little cramps in my stomach."*

Even before Patrick could reply to this, Brian couldn't hold it anymore. He let out a burst of hot air, making a considerably loud noise. Even the horses neighed to the noise.

"Brian is that what you call a little cramp, it sounded more like an ox being choked to death."

Brian replied, *"Sorry, Captain. I couldn't hold it in any longer."*

And sure enough, the awful smell started to invade the coach. Patrick concluded, *"There's no possible way that your god-awful smell is the result of my mother's banana bread. My God, I'm going to be sick. This was not part of the plan, Brian. I am going to kill you later."*

They heard some people conversing in Arabic. Both became very silent. They could recognize Ahmed's voice. The door of the coach opened, and Ahmed was the first to step in, but as soon as he was in, he stepped back out and mumbled something bad in Arabic.

Since the coachman didn't speak or understand Arabic, Ahmed repeated it in English, *"Did anyone clean this coach before coming to get us?"*

The coachman was startled by his reaction, so he decided to go and see for himself.

"Oh lord, what is that smell," the coachman coughed and then proceeded with an excuse, *"One of my horses might have a digestive problem."*

Ahmed replies, *"Maybe. You might want to watch what you're feeding them."*

Ahmed told everyone to get in and open the shutters. Hopefully, the wind would make the smell go away once they are on the road.

Sabah was a bit concerned. There was no sign of Brian or Patrick, and she was doubtful that there could have been a problem or else they would have been here by now. *"Maybe they're already here, and had a chance to sneak in the coach,"* she thought. But she needed to confirm this somehow. Since Sabah was the last one to get in, she purposely dropped her bag on the floor and bent down to pick it up.

She then knocked twice near the double floor of the carriage while saying something to her dad so the boys would know that she was the one knocking. Before she fully stood up, she heard two knocks loud enough to confirm the boys were inside the coach. She could not help but smile, which went away instantly as she entered the coach. The odor made her nauseous, as well as the people inside. Everyone had their noses covered with a scarf or a cloth. They gestured her to sit down, convincing her that the scent would go away the minute they started moving. Everyone was on board, and the stagecoach was on its way. The next stop was Tetouan. Of course, that entirely depended on the fact that everything went according to the plan.

Meanwhile, in Tetouan, Mohammed was about to head out for Tangier to pick up some medical supplies. Right when he was about to leave, Fatima came running out of the house to ask him if she could join him for the ride. She said she wanted to pick up some supplies that were not readily available in Tetouan. Mohammed said *"Yes, of course,"* with gratitude. It was a long journey, and he would certainly enjoy the company on the way.

Although Mohammed found Fatima's request slightly unusual. He didn't realize that the actual reason behind Fatima's sudden impulse to accompany him on the trip was to surprise and meet with the man of her dreams. Sabah had told Fatima at the International Trade Show that Patrick would be in Tangier this Saturday. But since she had no

181

means of communication and was unaware of Sabah's plan, Fatima simply manipulated an opportunity to meet with the man that presently invaded her dreams. Although Sabah's plan might have potentially failed with Fatima getting ready to leave for Tangier, there was still hope. There was only one road that led to Tangier, so it was highly plausible that they would meet their stagecoach heading for Tetouan.

An hour into the ride from Tangier, the two coaches crossed each other's path and immediately stopped in their tracks. The road was wide enough so that both coaches could stand next to each other without any difficulty. Mohammed jumped down from his coach and opened the door to the other so that he could greet everyone inside. Patrick and Brian were a little confused and were wondering what was going on out there.

The boys heard another person get off from Mohammed's coach, who happened to be standing quite close to them. As soon as this person walked closer towards their coach, they heard the person begin a conversation with Sabah. Brian recognized her voice instantly. The other voice belonged to none other than Fatima.

Brian turned to Patrick and whispered the words, *"Hey, it's Fatima."*

Patrick looked at him, uncertain and asked, *"Are you sure?"*

Patrick couldn't recognize Fatima's voice since he had still not had a one-on-one conversation with her yet.

Brian nodded his head in confirmation, *"I am sure that's Fatima's voice. I can recognize her voice very easily since I have spoken to her a couple of times."*

Patrick felt a little jealous at that, but more than that, he was worried.

He said, *"What is she doing here? You do realize that if she's here, traveling somewhere else, we're going all the way to Tetouan for nothing."*

Brian sniggered, *"Nope. Not really. The way I see it, you're the one who's on his way to Tetouan for nothing."*

Patrick huffed, *"Thank you for that astute observation; you blaggard."*

Patrick was not wonderfully comfortable with the situation at hand. He definitely had to come up with another plan in the next few minutes, or all of their endeavors would have been for nothing.

Suddenly, Patrick came up with an idea and nudged Brian with his elbow saying, *"All we have to do is sneak out of this coach and get into the other one without getting spotted."*

Brian looked at Patrick judgingly and did not like the idea at all.

Patrick looked at Brian with a convincing expression of authority, *"And that's an order. Don't forget that even while I'm lying down on the floor of a stagecoach next to you, I'm still your captain, and you would be wise to do my bidding."*

Brian was a little taken aback. He didn't expect Patrick to use his authority as a captain in this situation. Brian was actually quite impressed with his quick reactive thinking because Brian was about to, flat out, refuse the proposition. He was now forced to give some thought to Patrick's new plan. To be realistic, they were in this scene together so Patrick could meet with Fatima. After Brian thought of it for a few seconds, he finally agreed to the idea, knowing that he had no other choice. Brian did express to Patrick while getting ready to open the hatch, *"You know that's blackmail, Iy."* Patrick replied with a smile, *"It worked, didn't it?"*

Brian opened the hatch to the double floor, stretched out to see how everyone was staged and could see if the other coach had a double floor. He pushed himself back in and described to Patrick what the situation looked like out there. Mohammed was in front of their coach's doorway, and Fatima had her back turned to Brian. The coachman was holding the door and facing Brian while he gathered a look outside the coach.

Once they were sure that there was a double floor in the other coach, the only possible way of climbing upon it was to sneak out and crawl along the side of their coach.

If they did get caught this would be considered highly disrespectful and a great insult towards the Arab culture.

Nevertheless, the boys would have to make their way in front of the horses while still laying low and sneak alongside the rear of the other coach to finally sneak into the double floor.

The only person who could possibly see them while they were making their way silently to the next coach was Fatima. Hence the reason for taking that route.

Being well aware that she wanted to meet Patrick at all costs, she would most probably not say a word to help the boys cross over.

Before going ahead with the plan, Brian took another look at the neighboring stagecoach and confirmed that although it looked like an older model, it should definitely have a double floor.

Patrick was the first to pull himself out of the coach, and Brian followed. They crept along the side of the stagecoach towards the front. Everything seemed to be going as they had imagined. Patrick and Brian had finally reached the front, and the horses stayed calm. Now they had to make their way to the other stagecoach without making any sound to avoid getting seen or heard by anyone. Patrick began crawling in front of the horses, and Brian was right behind him. As Patrick made his way between the coaches, Fatima saw him squirm towards her stagecoach and let out a sound that startled everyone. She was so loud that Patrick heard her too.

He lifted his head up slowly and looked her right in the eyes. It made Patrick freeze like he was put into a spell. Brian saw Patrick's reaction and realized that he had seen Fatima for the first time in broad daylight. He was glad that his friend was finally looking at the woman he loved. But Brian knew this wasn't the time to stop crawling. He had started to worry a bit and wasn't sure what might happen if they didn't move in the next few seconds. He gave Patrick a push, but this made the horses nervous. The coachman could see that the horses were nervous and reacting to something, so he turned around to see why the horses were agitated.

When Fatima saw the coachman begin to turn around, she knew she had to do something quick so that Patrick would not be seen. Before the coachman had completely turned around, Fatima slapped him on the head. The coachman swiveled his head back and looked at Fatima, rubbing his head with his hand where she had hit him. He looked at her with a startled and confused look. Fatima judged his expression and explained that he had a big horsefly walking on his head and was probably ready to rip a piece of skin off his skull. Fatima held onto his attention long enough to give Patrick the time to crawl behind Fatima's carriage.

The commotion had caught Mohammed's attention. He turned away from the coach to look at what was going on. Fatima then saw Brian crawling right behind Patrick to get himself to the other side. Mohammed looked at Fatima and asked her what was going on. Fatima giggled while explaining the horsefly story to her brother. Meanwhile, the distraction had secured Patrick's passage to her carriage. Mohammed then stretched out a bit, and it was his turn to try and find out why the horses were agitated when Fatima let out a scream and smacked her brother, really hard, on the back of the head. Knowing that Brian was right behind Patrick, and he might not have had enough time to cross over, this seemed to be the perfect distraction. It worked the first time.

Mohammed looked at Fatima, clearly truly angry.

"What did you do that for?"

Fatima replied, *"You had a horsefly too. I guess it's horsefly season."*

Mohammed was still looking at Fatima with angry eyes while rubbing the back of his head. He did not really look convinced that there was a horsefly.

Both Brian and Patrick finally made it to the other coach with a lot of help from Fatima, and now that the coast was clear, they walked along the rear side and got into the other stagecoach. They then quietly shut the door. Once they were inside, they realized it was extremely uncomfortable compared to the one they were in previously.

The compartment was the same size as the other coach, but the inside was wet and humid as if it had sat outside in the rain. But other than this little detail, Patrick was thrilled that the plan worked out. All they had to do now was enjoy the ride until they got to their destination, wherever that may be!

Upon knowing that the two boys were in her coach, Fatima took Mohammed's place in front of the door and offered Sabah to come with them to Tangier. Sabah, still thinking the boys were in her coach, suggested to Fatima that it would be a better idea if Fatima would join her family for the trip to Tetouan. This exchange went on and on until Fatima became seriously impatient and took Sabah by the hand to pull her out of her seat, and then forcing her out of the coach. Everyone saw Fatima's aggression but thought nothing of it. It was merely a girl's quarrel for them. She then asked Sabah if she had brought any bags with her while heading to the coach's rear. As Fatima got to the back of the stagecoach, she bent down, pulled Sabah down by her arm, and opened the double floor compartment.

Sabah was surprised when she saw the compartment empty, but she instantly understood why Fatima was so insistent. Sabah went back to her coach to tell Ahmed that she had decided that she would be leaving with Fatima and would join them later on for dinner. Ahmed agreed and told Mohammed to take good care of their daughter. Mohammed nodded his head and assured him not to worry. He closed the coach's door, and off they went.

Mohammed got back into his own coach and told the girls to get inside and enjoy the ride. When Sabah got close to the coach, she bent down and knocked on the double floor, just as she had done before leaving Tangier. Brian recognized the signal, so he knocked back. Sabah was relieved to hear the knock and walked into the coach with a grin on her face. They were now on their way back to Tangier. There were minor hiccups in the plan due to unforeseen circumstances, but the results had been profitable so far. All four of them were in the same coach, and soon Patrick and Fatima could finally meet again. Nothing could possibly go wrong now.

The ride was a bit bumpy on the way back to Tangier, and the girls were having fun with the boys. They were stamping their feet on the floor while the boys were replying with knocks now and then. Everything was going well until suddenly, the coach crossed a huge hole in the road, which caused the double floor to crack open. The floor, being waterlogged, was weak and couldn't support the two boys' weight when it wheeled over this huge pothole. The floor opened up a good six inches, and the boy's feet were exposed. They started knocking faster on the bottom of the floor to indicate something was wrong, but both Fatima and Sabah thought that the boys were playing, so they kept on giggling.

Patrick looked at Brian, saying, *"They think we're having fun."*

Brian replied, *"Yeah. We have got to find a way out of here."* As Brian opened the door to the compartment, Patrick looked at him, saying, *"You're not going to jump out, are you?"* and Brian replied, *"Of course not, that would be insane. But if we can slip out and grab on to the back of the coach, we might be able to have a safe ride back to Tangier. If we stay here, this floor will collapse before we arrive."*

Brian finished talking and reached out to the edge of the coach to slip himself out. However, the coach ran into a bigger pothole, bigger than the previous one, sending the whole floor crashing to the ground with Patrick and Brian on it. The racket was awful, and the girls became worried for the boys. They both got down to the floor, pounding and waiting for a reply. When there was no reply, they each chose a window to look outside. They pulled their heads outside to see the boys literally drifting on the double floor like a sled.

It was as if they were sailing on a raft, but instead of being on the water, they were on a dirt road. Mohammed had heard the noise and was trying to slow down the coach, coming to a stop to see what had happened. The boy's little raft had eventually come to a stop, and that, before the coach did. The boys turned over and sat down, facing the rear end of the coach. But as soon as they saw the coach come to a stop, they knew they couldn't stay there, or else Mohammed would most definitely see them and that couldn't happen. They both stood up and ran into the bushes on the right side of the road then crouched down behind them to hide. Mohammed got off and looked underneath the stagecoach. All he could see was a huge hole and the missing luggage compartment.

He asked the girls to stay inside the carriage as he walked towards the floor of his carriage that had fallen to the ground. When he saw the wooden floor on the ground, he squatted down to take a closer look and understood that the floor had collapsed because the wood had absorbed a lot of moisture, but what he could not understand were the two faint human-like prints on the wooden floor.

Shaking his head, he told himself that this could not be possible. *"I seriously need to take some time off,"* Mohammed said as he rejected the thought. He outright rejected the belief of having people stored away in his lugged compartment. He could not do much about the hole in his carriage at that time. He pushed the sled-like wooden floor into the bushes so that another coach wouldn't run over it and get hurt. Luckily for the boys, Mohammed pushed the floor on the opposite side of the road from where they were hiding. Before he made his way back to the carriage, thinking that he would have to build a new luggage compartment when he returned home. Patrick was waiting impatiently for Mohammed to get back onto the coach because he had, just then, come up with another plan. As Mohammed walked back, Patrick quickly explained to Brian that the minute Mohammed would pull himself onto the coach, they would have to make a run for the rear of the carriage and sit there for the rest of the trip. Brian had been having the same thought and agreed without any hesitation.

Mohammed was back at the coach and noticed the worried look on the girl's faces. He decided to give them an explanation about what had happened, but little did he know that they weren't interested in the luggage compartment. The boys were getting ready to make a run for the coach but suddenly, Brian let out an *"Ouch."* He wriggled and turned around, glared at Patrick, and whispered, *"Why did you pinch me? He's not on the coach yet, we can't go now."*

Patrick gave Brian a startled look and said, *"What? I haven't even touched you."* Brian was very surprised and slightly confused by Patrick's response. He started looking around to find the cause of the pinch he had felt. Patrick didn't know what Brian was searching for, but he became concerned and decided to look around as well.

This time, it was Patrick's turn to feel a nasty burn at the rear of his right leg. The impact made him squirm. He turned around towards Brian while rubbing the back of his leg and said with his teeth crimped, *"Why did you pinch me? I told you before ... I didn't touch you."* Brian was shocked and replied. *"Mate, I didn't touch you either."*

Patrick's eyebrows rose up. He retorted, *"Then who did?"* before Patrick could finish his sentence, Brian had pushed the bush aside to find a colony of red ants. Brian realized that the ants had bitten them. The vermin had tasted their flesh, and they would indeed come back for more. Patrick, on the other hand, had not seen the colony of red ants. He was mostly looking out for the coach to make a timely run for it the second it started moving. As Brian got ready to share his discovery, Patrick turned to Brian and tugged his shirt at shoulder height, saying, *"Now's the time. The coach is leaving."*

There was no time to explain, so Brian stood up and started running with Patrick. While running, Patrick had to slow down. He had been bitten multiple times again. Brian, slightly behind Patrick, also had the same problem. The action of running had indeed agitated the ants, and as the boys slowed down while continuously slapping their bums, groins, and legs, Brian informed Patrick about the colony of red ants. The girls were watching the boys twitching and slapping away and they were indeed very confused about what was going on. They noticed that the coach was getting further away from the boys and that they wouldn't have a chance to catch up.

When Patrick discovered that he was getting bitten by red ants, he got terrified and stopped running. He was panic-stricken, and at that moment, he took all his clothes off. Everything was off except for his underpants. Then, while squirming, he tried to swipe and killed all the ants he had on him, at least the ones he could see or feel. Brian came to a stop as well and had to do exactly the same thing.

The boys had to help each other out by swiping the ants they couldn't reach on their backs. Once it was all over, they both looked at the road in front of them to see that the coach was nowhere in sight.

"Well, so much for sticking to the plan."

Patrick said disappointingly. Brian didn't say a word as he turned his pants inside and out before putting them back on. Although back to back failures were looking to be their fate, Brian came up with another idea. He asked Patrick how far he thought they were from Tangier. Patrick estimated that their walking distance was about an hour away. Brian then suggested that if they jogged fast enough, they might be able to reach Tangier before the girls made their way back to Tetouan. But they would have to find the girls once they were back in Tangier.

Patrick cried out loud, *"Hell, what else can go wrong; it's worth a try. It's not like I'm busy or anything."* So, the boys, feeling the burn from the ant bites, started jogging as fast as they could to Tangier.

Within an hour, they were minutes away from the city, and even though they were in pain, exhausted and drained from all the jogging, they gathered their strength and made one last run to the marketplace. They hoped that the girls would be there as this was the most obvious place to find them. As they ran into the marketplace, they saw their stagecoach at the other end of the road. Unluckily for them, it was actually leaving. The boys were extremely tired, drained entirely of their energy. They were way too exhausted to make another effort to catch up to it.

They both bent down, grabbed their knees with their hands, and tried to catch their breath out of fatigue as they watched the coach making its way back to Tetouan.

Patrick looked at Brian and brooded, *"How many times do I have to run after this coach before I can finally meet her again."*

Brian replied, *"I don't know. I guess as many times as it takes, partner!"*

Weeks passed by. The two friends made persevering attempts so that Patrick and Fatima could finally meet another time, but fate was not yet ready for them to have them meet. Patrick and Brian tried everything humanly possible, but life was not favoring this reunion.

Their patience and strength weakened, but their love and passion grew stronger as they followed their hearts into the abyss of love. And both of them knew how much they yearned for this love to grow. They had both personally vowed never to stop making efforts or creating possibilities to meet for just another time. Patrick would have to continue to tug on, as hard as he could, holding onto that rope of hope, believing that he would soon unite with Fatima.

Although trying to pressure the hand of fate, all they really had to do was let nature take its course, but they were both eager to finally sit next to each other and talk to each other at length. They were both living the same dream and eventually, life would have to give in letting destiny follow its course.

As long as there was hope, they were able to embrace the fact that they would join hands again one day soon.

Chapter 14
A Change in Priorities

A few weeks later, in Fez, morning came about with a bright sun and a fresh little breeze that caressed the flowers, causing their scents to spread throughout the land. Fatima woke up early that morning with a big smile on her face, the reason for which even she wasn't entirely sure of. All she knew was that her heart was filled with love today and that she couldn't stop thinking about Patrick. No matter how much she tried to let go of her thoughts. She would imagine herself loving the man of her dreams as far as her imagination could take her.

Her sister had been away with her husband and they were not expected back until tomorrow. Fatima had all the liberty to express herself freely, and that she did. Fatima was presently in the kitchen busy preparing breakfast when Hanane walked in. She knew Fatima very well. When she saw her smiling, she knew that there was a good reason behind it. She just didn't know what it was, yet. However, it was true, that they both haven't seen much of each other lately. What could have happened that made her cousin so giddy, Hanane wondered. Too curious to know, she couldn't help herself anymore and had to pose the question.

"Okay, that's enough now, Fatima. I must know... You've been grinning nonstop, and I cannot contain my curiosity any longer. I can't remember the last time I've seen you so cheerful and jolly. Tell me, what is going on with you? What is making you so happy?"

Hanane didn't have to do a lot of convincing to find out the reason. And from the looks of it, Fatima was dying to tell Hanane her little secret. She jumped at Hanane's request, clapped her hands, and told her about this man she had met. Hanane was surprised and instantly matched up with Fatima's energy level.

She exclaimed with delight as Fatima narrated about the festival and the trade show and the coach incident. Hanane was extremely happy for Fatima and was very curious at the same time. She had so many questions for Fatima.

As soon as Fatima took a pause, Hanane fired them one after the other, and Fatima answered all of them very patiently. She asked about how Patrick looked, what he does, about his family, and so on. They talked and laughed while making up scenarios amongst themselves where Hanane would play the role of Patrick and act in the most romantic way. She would ask Fatima for her hand, kneeling down as she proposed to her dramatically. Not realizing that their chatter and laughter were so loud, they eventually woke up their nieces. Karima and Samira entered the kitchen, rubbing their eyes. As soon as they saw their two aunts having such an animated conversation, their curiosity spiked up. They certainly wanted to know the story too.

Fatima trusted her nieces more than anyone in the world after Hanane. She was sure that they would never snitch on their aunt in consequence of breaking her trust. They loved her so much that they would never do anything to bring her any harm. Thus, she told her nieces the whole story about her experience with love at first sight.

They were happy for Fatima, and it was their turn to fire questions one after another. She took a deep breath and began answering their questions too, with a smile that could not deny happiness. It was clear that answering all these questions were tiring and exhausting for Fatima. Yet she was enjoying it too. While sharing her joyful adventure, it made it feel so real and closer to her. This was her fantasy land fairytale coming to life. They were all together in the kitchen, gossiping together and fantasizing, and time flew in such a way that they even had forgotten to prepare breakfast. Their chit-chat all came to a halt when they heard someone knocking at the door. Fatima stepped out of the kitchen to see who it was. It was her nieces' private English teacher, Miss Teak.

Fatima opened the door and tensely explained to Miss Teak that they were running a bit off schedule because they had slept in. To make up for their lateness, Fatima invited her to have breakfast with them. Miss Teak clearly understood their situation and agreed to join them. Since Layla was away for a few days, things were much easier around the house for everyone.

That same afternoon, during Karima and Samira's lessons, their teacher realized that Samira was not feeling well. After their reading session, Samira went straight to her room to lay down. Miss Teak, before leaving their residence, went to see Fatima so she could relay her concern regarding Fatima's little niece. Fatima was very thankful to her for sharing this concern and ran upstairs to see Samira. The moment Fatima entered the room, she saw Karima sitting by her sister's side, and realized something was wrong as she walked closer towards Samira. Fatima held her hand and touched her forehead. It was burning. Fatima was worried about Samira and decided to run to the stables to speak with her brother, Mohammed about it. Without wasting any time, Mohammed readied the horses and coach and headed out to Asdeen's house.

Asdeen was a doctor and a very close friend of the family. As he arrived at Layla's house with Mohammed, he made his way up to Samira's room. After examining her, he wasn't really sure of her illness. It looked like a cold, but he explained to Fatima that there was a bacterium that was spreading around. It attacked the lungs and made it difficult to breathe.

There was no known cure for the bacteria. Asdeen, being incredibly careful in his choice of words with Fatima, told her that in some cases the bacteria led to death. Fatima remained calm, thinking that it was probably a cold. As Asdeen left the house, he explained the stages of the sickness to Fatima. If Samira showed any of those symptoms, it would mean that she was developing the infection. That night, Fatima and Hanane spent the night in Samira's room, taking turns to look for any apparent symptoms of the bacteria. Karima wanted to be of help too, but Fatima told Karima that they weren't really sure what Samira's illness was and that she should better sleep in her room. Fatima laid down beside Samira, gently passing her fingers through her hair as she hummed a melody, she had learned for her nieces to put them to sleep. Fatima forgot the title of this melody, but she called it *"The Angel's Lullaby."*

Early the next morning, Fatima woke up feeling a bit guilty for falling asleep. She rushed to have a look at Samira and Fatima was wishing with all her heart for her condition to be just a cold, but as she set eyes on Samira, she was definitely going through the stages of the illness that Asdeen had told her about. The realization of the illness made Fatima terribly upset.

She tried not to panic as she ran outside to look for Mohammed so he could call Asdeen back as fast as possible. Her brother didn't waste any time and rushed to the doctor's house. Fatima went back upstairs to reassess Samira's condition, making sure that her judgment about the illness wasn't just her imagination playing tricks on her. Once she got back to Samira's room, she tip-toed to the bed and put her ear on Samira's chest. She could hear a restrictive sound of air going through her lungs. Her hand brushed against Samira's arm while lifting her head off her chest and Fatima felt a little moisture upon her skin. Samira was sweating due to fever. Fatima woke up Hanane to look after Samira while she went downstairs to prepare something to bring the fever down. Hanane agreed and went to look after Samira. As Fatima was walking downstairs, all she could think about was to get things under control. She tried not to panic while praying that this ordeal had come to a good ending.

Fatima had assembled a few fresh cloths with a big bowl of cool water. She had also pulled out a few vegetables to prepare a soup later on. Just when Fatima was about to walk back upstairs, Layla walked into the house with her husband. She greeted Fatima with a big smile and began telling her what a wonderful time they had in Marrakesh. Fatima had no time to lose and quickly explained to Layla that she was happy that she had a good time, but she had more pressing matters to look after than to listen to her adventures. Layla felt very insulted by the way Fatima greeted her. Her husband was even more surprised by her behavior.

While Fatima walked up the stairway, she realized she had been very harsh with Layla.

"I'm really sorry about the rudeness; it's just ... Samira is very ill, Layla ... "

Samira was extremely sick? Upon hearing this, Layla rushed to the top of the stairway. She almost ran her sister down in the process and then rushed into the room to see her daughter. Her husband assumed that sick meant nothing serious, so he went outside to unpack the coach.

Fatima entered the room and saw her sister dramatizing the situation without even knowing what was going on. Little did she know that she would soon be living the shock of her life. Layla began accusing everyone for her daughter's condition. She was assuming it was everyone's fault that Samira had fallen sick. Fatima finally got a chance to explain the situation to Layla.

Once Layla learned about the consequences of the illness, she was stunned for a moment. Snapping from her daze, she started to scream and expressed her rage at everyone because they weren't intelligent enough to get Asdeen over here to take care of Samira but as she finished her sentence, Asdeen walked into the room. Layla, hypocritically, took a more refined attitude towards everyone when Asdeen was present in the room. Her looks and what people thought about her were of great value to her if you happened to be bourgeois.

Asdeen examined Samira, and even though he wanted to give some good news to Layla, he couldn't. Samira had the infection, and there was nothing he could do to cure it. As the doctor explained to Layla that Samira had no chance of coming back from this illness, she became hysterical. She grabbed him, then took hold of Hanane and then Fatima and yelled, *"No, this is not possible."* Fatima freed herself and held on to her emotions. She asked Asdeen if there was any possible way that this illness could be treated. Asdeen replied that there could be another way to deal with this, but it had nothing to do with medicine.

At this point, he definitely had been able to direct everyone's attention to himself. He explained to the ladies that there was a gypsy-like figure who lived among the poor endowed with a gift for healing.

"He would probably be the best chance of saving Samira, but let me also add that as a doctor, I don't hold his pseudo-scientific practice to a reliable ground, nor do I approve of

it." the doctor, slightly affirming himself.

Fatima promptly asked Asdeen for his name. The doctor replied, *"Moustapha."* Fatima was struck with a flashback of a moment at the market with Layla. She turned around and looked at Layla, telling her that she knew the man and might be able to find him. With a bit of inspiration, Layla told Hanane to leave with Fatima to find this man. Once outside, Mohammed was given the destination, and off they went.

While Fatima was on her way to the marketplace, she couldn't stop thinking of the day Layla had spat on Moustapha. She wondered about the kind of reaction he would have once he saw Layla again. She didn't talk about that matter with Layla before leaving the house, but she knew that if she found Moustapha and he turned out to be the man she quarreled with, Layla would be in for a big surprise.

Fatima and Hanane arrived at the marketplace and split up. They knew that they had a better chance to find Moustapha if each of them searched for him separately. They asked everyone if they had seen Moustapha, but no one seemed to know where he was. All the merchants seemed to be repeating the same thing. He moved around a lot like a nomad while helping people, so he never stayed in the same place for a very long time. For all they knew, he could also be in another village or another city altogether. Walking down the street, Hanane watched children gathered around a man sharing a bread pie with them. She had a hunch that might be Moustapha. She felt shy about approaching him directly, so she ran out to look for Fatima and brought her to where the man sat with the children.

Fatima looked at Hanane and heaved a sigh of relief. She told her that this man was indeed Moustapha, and was glad that the merchants were wrong, as she had hoped they would be. Fatima sent Hanane to buy fresh fruits and almonds for the children using the money Layla had given her. Fatima was convinced this would be a nice offering for the children and the right thing to do for someone asking for help.

Fatima walked up to Moustapha and excused her intrusion regarding the children. She told the children to remain seated for a while longer because they would be getting fresh fruits and almonds. Moustapha was an incredibly wise man and, without looking at Fatima, continued to share his bread.

"You give with the need to receive, my child," he said with a smile. Fatima was surprised by his reaction. She didn't know it would be so obvious, but she didn't have any time to waste either. Fatima was very honest with him and quickly agreed with Moustapha, who handed out the last pieces of bread to the kids and did not keep any for himself.

Moustapha turned around to face Fatima, took her hands in his, and bowed down to kiss them. Bringing his head up, he told Fatima that he knew they would meet again. Fatima got a glimpse of his eyes, and what she saw surprised her. Noticing Fatima's puzzled expression, Moustapha told her, *"Do not be alarmed, child. This is only a little physical unbalance of life."*

Fatima didn't want to show any reaction to what he was saying, but she knew that she wouldn't succeed in hiding much from a man like Moustapha. He had an enlightened air about him that was hard to ignore. Fatima felt amazingly comfortable around him. She explained Samira's illness, and as he had predicted, Fatima had a favor to ask. Without hearing the story to the end, Moustapha got up from his place and asked Fatima to lead the way to where the sick child was.

In that instance, Hanane came down the road with the fruits and almonds that Fatima had asked her to purchase. She distributed them among the children and left. As they approached the little palace, Layla ran outside, leaving her husband with Samira. She thought that she would greet the healer with all the riches in the world to save her daughter. That was exactly when the conflict began.

The carriage came to a halt, and Moustapha recognized Layla without even getting out of the carriage. After Hanane walked out of the carriage, Moustapha grabbed Fatima by the arm, asking her to take him back to the marketplace. Fatima did not need an explanation for his behavior. She knew that he had recognized her sister, but she had hoped that Moustapha was wise enough to surpass and forget about his mishap with Layla.

Fatima turned around and explained she could not take him back. It wasn't because of her sister's authority, but because of her love for Samira. Moustapha felt he had been cheated by Fatima, knowing that she had witnessed the incident her sister had put on display a while back at the marketplace. But after the explanation she gave, he felt Fatima's love for the child and was reassured of Fatima's purity. Moustapha came out of the carriage. Layla, upon seeing Moustapha, looked at Fatima and Hanane and turned red. She bellowed out that they had brought a beggar to the house, not a savior. Fatima decided to stand up to her sister and implored her to see things as they were for once in her life and to stop being mean to people whom she judged were beneath her in some way.

Moustapha looked up at Fatima and told her that he could not do anything to change Layla's fate. And if things were as bad as they were, life had a reason to make it this way. He added, in a sorrowful tone of voice, *"If no one could escort me back to the marketplace, I will go back on foot."* He turned around to make his way back to the market.

The three women looked at Moustapha, walking away and as if Moustapha's deception wasn't enough, it began to rain. Hanane ran back to the house while looking at Layla with disgust on her face for the way she had treated Moustapha. Fatima grabbed her sister's arms and shook them with a lot of force. Layla had no shame for what she had done. Provoked by her indifference, Fatima yelled at her, *"I hope you can live with yourself after realizing that your values in life will be the reason for your daughter's death!"*

213

Fatima, with tears in her eyes, left her sister alone to join Hanane. Her last words were heavy to absorb, but Layla was very strong-headed and turned around to go back into the house. As she got closer to the door, Layla started to feel the pain and agony of imagining her daughter's death. Deep down inside her; she knew she had to give in to herself and sacrifice a few of her unacceptable values. She could not live with the thought of losing her daughter, especially knowing she had a chance to save her.

As she came to cross the door, she stopped herself from going inside and succumbed to her conscience. Like good winning over evil, life had successfully proven a point. She quickly turned around and sprinted out to catch up to the beggar.

As she ran to catch up to Moustapha, she burst into tears, realizing how dreadful she was and hoped to God that this man she called a beggar would give her a chance to redeem herself. When Layla finally caught up to Moustapha, she knelt down before him in the mud and begged him to heal her daughter. Moustapha came to a stop and looked down towards the lady with the raging heart. Moustapha was indeed a healer and one with a forgiving soul. This is what is most needed in order to heal, forgiveness. And so, as he looked down upon his foe, he reflected his thoughts towards reason.

Looking down at Layla, he put his hand on her head and said, *"Seeing you kneel before a beggar should be enough suffering for a lady of your stature."* Bringing Layla to a stand, he said, *"Let me now kneel before you for the suffering I have caused."* As Moustapha knelt before her, she embraced the man before he could kneel down to the floor. She told him that he was too great a man for him to kneel before her feet. Moustapha, who was now proud of his decision, looked at her, and said, *"A healing is waiting for our arrival."* Layla broke into a little chuckle while the tears were still streaming down her cheeks.

Without wasting any more time, Moustapha and Layla headed back to the palace.

Chapter 15
The Daydream

Layla had asked Fatima to stay close to the house after Samira's healing. It was awful to see her like this, but Samira was slowly recuperating. Her condition was getting better as the days passed by. Fatima's love for Samira was a testament to being her favorite niece. Their bond was strong due to Samira being Layla's firstborn, and the first baby Fatima had ever held so near and dear.

Samira had grown up to be a beautiful, healthy, intelligent girl. Other than a common cold, she had never fallen sick or had any health issues. Perhaps this was the reason her sickness had shocked everyone senseless. Fatima made sure to be by Samira's side, ensuring she had everything she needed for a prompt recovery.

Amid Samira's bedridden state, Fatima hadn't stepped out of the house for a while. She wasn't able to go anywhere in case Samira might need her. This unfortunate incident had unwillingly put aside the man she cared for and made it difficult to make any plans to meet him again. The days seemed to last forever, and hours felt like days. All this time spent aiding others to get through these harsh times, she had inadvertently forgotten herself. Despite that, there wasn't a day that she didn't think of the man she held dear to her heart.

Fatima was getting tired of all the chores. She would clean the house, disinfect the bathroom, scrub the floors, cook meals, and clean the kitchen while monitoring Samira's condition. One such afternoon, Fatima had just finished doing the laundry and was hanging the clothes out to dry. After hanging the laundry, she sat down against the large brick wall of the house to catch her breath.

She closed her eyes and allowed the calming heat of the sun to caress her face. She had felt a sudden calmness while sitting there; her fatigue from overworking was fading away. A few minutes later, she had dozed off into a deep sleep. A couple of minutes into her sleep, she began to dream and later wished this would be real.

She was levitating inside a mass of deep white fog. The fog was so intense that she felt like it was a part of her or emanating from within her. Fatima hovered around in the clouds on a floor that she couldn't see but felt beneath her feet. She had never felt so light and relaxed as she did at that moment. Suddenly, her heart started to beat at a nervous pace, which brought back the memory of the first time she had met the man of her dreams. Momentarily blinded by the clouds and the wisp surrounding her, Fatima anxiously looked around her, while her intuition tingling, signaling Patrick was near.

From a levitation position, it was like if something had tugged her from below. Shortly afterwards, she felt a sensation that she was falling from the sky but lightly as a feather. Fatima suddenly fell beneath the clouds to see that she had landed in Patrick's arms. Confused, she looked around to see where they were. She could hear the sound of the waves and feel the moisture in the air that embraced her skin. She then realized they were both sailing in the middle of the sea.

Being alone on the ship, they shared their feelings and emotions without any timidity or concerns. Time was like an hourglass, but the sand did not flow, symbolizing that time was completely unaware of their existence. The sails were deployed even though there was no trace of wind. Only stillness hung all around, except for a breeze of desire, passing while they embraced, and held each other closely.

The world darkened regardless of the timelessness of the moment, and nightfall did come about. The moon was but a silver disc in the sky, which felt infinite, and it was at that still, sensuous moment that the gleam in their eyes, hinted for a kiss. Achingly slow, they both moved in and swaddled their lips, with each other's lip.

The passion grew stronger, as their hearts beat louder, but after the kiss broke, their eyes fluttered, as they opened to see each other bewitched. And with that look, they gazed into each other's soul, but they soon realized that they were in a different space. Overcome by flowers on the deck in a moonlight filled with love and desire. Fatima held Patrick's hand and led him towards an area where they could lie.

Caressing each other without a touch, conveyed that love meant so much, and all were being understood with just a simple thought. But as desires grew stronger, the waves got rougher and with nothing more than the air separating their skin from each other's caress, a thick fog surrounded them, and the sea became calmer. Little raindrops started tumbling from a sky that was not and entered the chamber's window. Fatima stretched her neck aiding her face to embrace the fresh rain. Her eyes flew open, pulling her out of this magnificent enchanting dream. It had started to rain outside where she sat, and a drizzle of rain had awakened her. Sheltering herself, she attempted, with all her might, to jump back into the dream. But it was useless.

Fatima broke into tears yearning for Patrick. She wanted to lie down with him, to be held and caressed. But all she could do was make her way back inside, out of the pouring rain, while wiping the tears on her veil.

Chapter 16
Brian's Misfortune

It was a normal evening in Gibraltar. The sun had set, and the sky was navy blue. Like all other days, Brian had arrived to work on time and had remained busy the entire day. He had a habit of ending his day at the usual pub. He wasn't much of a drinker; he only drank occasionally, but he liked being at the Green Sail Pub, surrounded by the hullabaloo. It was much better than spending an evening with his father.

His father, Mr. Fuller, constantly complained about anything and everything in life, no matter how big or how small it was. Every time Brian was around his father, or if both were in the same room, Mr. Fuller would bring up one of three subjects for sure.

The first subject was how bad his life was treating him and how it was never fair; number two, how sick and unwell he was, number three, money, or the lack of it.

According to Mr. Fuller, he never had enough money, even though Brian would regularly give him much more than he needed. His father would get quite happy when Brian gave him money, and he never really questioned Brian about where he was getting it from. He only considered that his son was a hard-working man, and Brian's father never allowed himself to learn about his son or what he did. He was more concerned with not getting any money than worrying about where it was coming from.

Mr. Fuller had become a heartless man. He was always thinking of ways to manipulate his son so that he would give him more and more money. But as they say, life has its own ways of putting things back into their place. And mostly, in the way, they were supposed to be in the first place.

Things at the pub were the same as usual. People would gather and tell their tales and anecdotes to each other. They would share the wildest stories and adventures with anyone gathered there who wanted to hear it. It seemed like a competition, a race for who could tell the most entertaining story.

It didn't matter if the story was true or not – the bigger and more outlandish the lie, the better and more crowd-pleasing the story was. There were so many occasions when most of the customers in the pub would have had a bit too much to drink. At times, the booze would flow like a river, and everyone would want to take a dip in it. During these times, breaking into a song followed naturally. People would start singing while some would even start dancing, usually those who weren't very good at it. The pub people couldn't carry a tune to save their lives, but they would still sing regardless, it was a natural reaction to their intoxication.

One really had the chance to see all the colorful people of Gibraltar at the pub.

It was still early, and even though Brian had to work the following day, he decided to stay for a bit longer. Everybody was in the mood for fun, and he wanted to allow himself some of that fun tonight.

Of course, all good things come to an end, but usually, the word "end" is defined differently. The little party at the pub came to an end when the hoodlums walked through the door. One could never be sure about the hoodlums. It was hard to tell when they felt like having fun or when they were not in the mood for it. They always carried a grim look on their faces, making everyone feel uneasy with their entrance.

Once they had settled in, a few of them crossed the bar and walked toward Brian. As they walked closer to where

Brian sat, he could detect that they were not there to have fun. They walked up next to Brian's seat and asked him if they could have a word outside with him for a minute.

Everyone else was surprised, shocked even. They were surprised because out of all the people, Brian was not the type of person who would be friends or have any ties with the thugs. Brian ignored everyone's shocked expressions and puzzled faces. He nodded to the hoodlums and walked behind them as they stepped outside the pub.

Brian did not see any danger in this situation because he didn't have anything to worry about. Or did he? He found the situation very alarming because he was sure that the hoodlums would never blow his cover in public or expose him in front of an audience. It wasn't their way of doing business.

Once they were outside, the hoodlums brought Brian close to their stagecoach by dragging his arms from either side. He struggled and tried to wriggle out, but it was of no use.

A member of the hoodlums was waiting patiently on top of the carriage. He kicked off a wooden box with full force.

It fell to the ground with a loud smash and broke. Brian glanced down and thought he knew what was going on. But then his eyes observed what was inside the box and he was shocked.

While all of this was going on, a customer walked out of the pub and neared the coach parked at the back of the Green Sail Pub. He was going to urinate against the wall. Apparently, he had too much to drink, or at least that's what he wanted to show the others present outside. He wobbled to imitate how badly he wanted to pee, but all he wanted to do was to see what was happening between Brian and the hoodlums.

The hoodlums shot the man a serious, menacing look, and he understood that he wasn't welcome there. So, he finished up and went back inside without saying a word.

The contents of the box were not what the hoodlums had paid Brian for, so it was clear that Brian was incredibly nervous upon seeing what was inside the box. He knew that this scenario wasn't going to end well, but he didn't know exactly what the thugs were going to do.

The situation with all its tension worsened when Brian saw the leader, Garra del Diablo, step out of the carriage. He was a heavy man with a ring on each of his fingers. Much to Brian's surprise, Garra was ready to negotiate. He explained to Brian that since they hadn't gotten the merchandise they had ordered, he would just have to give Garra del Diablo his money back, and everybody could go on with their lives.

The leader assured him that no one would get hurt, but Brian now had a bigger problem to worry about. The merchandise in question was highly paid for, and he had already given all the money to his father. He tried explaining to them that he didn't have the money, but he promised that he would try to get most of it back. He requested that he just needed some time to get it back.

Garra did not like Brian's response. He wasn't at all happy with his reaction. He started cracking his knuckles, and all his rings glinted under the lowly lit backyard. Brian wasn't taking him seriously, he thought. Diablo had found out that Brian was in charge of security on the ship, and the merchandise had lost him a lot of money. He could not figure out how they could have received the wrong merchandise if Brian had not deceived him on purpose. He knew that Brian must have checked the box before putting it aside. Brian couldn't figure the mishap out either. He yet kept on explaining that he didn't do it on purpose but still left his father out of the explanation. As time passed, his nervousness grew stronger. He figured that the situation was getting more complicated than it had set out to be. The leader went from a negotiable to a non-negotiable mood when he suspected that it was nothing but lies coming out of Brian's mouth. Brian didn't know what to do.

Fearing for his life, the only thing that came to his mind was to make a run for it. He didn't think it through, though. The hoodlums had already predicted he was going to do something like that. As soon as he was about to take off, they moved ahead and grabbed him.

Garra del Diablo let out a loud, merciless laugh that was dripping with sarcasm. His belly flopped up and down with his laughter.

"Boys, I think Brian should learn to show us a little respect. Why don't you give him a quick lesson," he told the hoodlums and stepped back into the stagecoach? As soon as the door of the coach closed behind the leader, the hoodlums leaped onto Brian and began beating him like a drum. They

thrashed him and continued until he spat out blood and was panting for his breath. Once they were done, they left Brian out on the street, his clothes and body smeared in blood. Watching him writhe in pain, satisfied were the hoodlums, and they got back into the coach. Garra del Diablo got out of the coach again and walked toward Brian. He showed no concern about Brian's mangled state.

He simply looked at him and said, *"We will come back tomorrow. You better not disappoint me again, Brian. I am hoping you'll have the money with you,"* he said. In less than a minute, Brian heard the coach ride away into the night.

Brian's eyes were swollen because of the beating. He was incapable of getting up. Every inch of his body was aching and pounding with pain, so he thought it would be best if he laid down for a bit in his blood and waited to regain some strength to get back up.

Meanwhile, at Catherine's house, Patrick had just finished dinner and was heading out to the Green Sail Pub. He wanted to meet Miguel and explain the new procedures he had come up with regarding the cargo and maybe catch the person responsible for all the stealing. Even though Brian was in charge of security, Patrick had realized that the situation was critical. So, he decided to swap labels from the more expensive cargo to the lower-valued ones. This would create a bad situation for the one who was stealing it, thought Patrick. He assumed that the person who ended up with the stolen goods might show up after getting the wrong merchandise. Patrick knew the commodities were worth a fortune, so obviously, someone was paying substantial sums of money for the goods.

Patrick was passing by the side of the Green Sail Pub when he heard a funny noise. He stopped in his tracks, backed up a little, and tried to listen where the sound was coming from. He was convinced that he could hear someone moaning. He followed the faint noise to the alley at the back of the pub. Turning around the corner, he recognized Brian's broken body lying half-unconscious on the ground, barely holding on to his life.

Patrick dashed towards Brian. When he got closer to his friend's body, he saw how bad his condition really was. Instantly, many questions went through his mind, but he suppressed them. Patrick bent down to help Brian get up, but it wasn't a simple task, Brian was in excruciating pain. Patrick understood that the beating was not a single man's work. What he didn't understand was why someone would do this to Brian. From where Patrick stood, Brian's condition required immediate medical attention. He didn't look good at all. Patrick had to call someone for help.

"I will have to leave you for a short while, my brother. You need a doctor, and my mother will know what to do," he told Brian.

Brian reached out his hand towards Patrick in disagreement. Waving his hand, he was asking him not to leave. Patrick became conflicted and had to push back tears. He didn't know what to do but decided to stay by his friend's side. He removed his shirt to wipe the blood off Brian's face. While doing that, Patrick realized that there was a serious amount of blood oozing out of Brian's mouth. This only meant one thing. Brian had suffered internal injuries. Patrick again tried to tell Brian that he needed to receive medical attention.

"You're in bad shape, brother, let me get my mother. Your bruises need tending, we need to stop that blood loss." Patrick bit his lips to suppress his tears. It was difficult to watch his best friend battered so brutally.

Brian felt his body growing cold and still begged Patrick to stay. Patrick felt a surge of anger and hate for the people who had done this to Brian. He simultaneously felt sad and hopeless toward his friend's rapidly deteriorating condition. He sat down next to Brian and pulled him carefully towards himself while attending to his wounds. Brian frailly tried to raise his head to talk to his friend, but Patrick told him to save his energy and lie still. *"I'm here with you. Nothing's going to happen. Just stay quiet."*

Brian had sensed something about his condition and knew it wasn't going to get any better. He felt it was important to confide in Patrick since he wasn't sure what might happen next. Brian gulped down the blood in his throat and began to tell Patrick his story.

His voice came out hoarsely, but Brian explained the whole truth about how he stole cargo off the ship to make some extra coin so his father could lead a better life. He also stole so that he could get his father the medical attention he needed. Patrick felt a mix of emotions. He was aware that Mr. Fuller always made Brian feel guilty for how his mother died, even though Brian didn't have anything to do with it. It was Mr. Fuller's way of getting rid of his aggravation and frustration toward his not-so-good-life. At the same time, he took advantage of Brian's kindness and trust to make his life more comfortable. Everybody knew that Mr. Fuller was not sick, he was simply a manipulative, torturing vulture who had never done anything for Brian, but in turn, he had made Brian's life miserable. Everyone knew this to be true, but all they ever did was sympathize and not say a word.

Brian kept on coughing and wheezing while he divulged everything. Brian tried to hold on to the last fragment of his life to apologize for the betrayal. His mouth filled up, and he coughed out loud, vomiting a mouthful of blood. Some of it splashed onto Patrick's face. As soon as he wiped the blood from his eyes and looked down at Brian, he saw him lying on the ground, lifeless and still, his eyes staring at the sky in horror. He was still bleeding from the various injuries he had sustained.

Patrick felt a shudder in his heart that crept to his whole body. His eyes glazed over, and his mouth dropped open. He shook him lightly at first, careful not to hurt him too much.

"Brian ... Brian?" No response. *"No, Brian. No."* He looked from left to right for help and shook his dead friend.

"Anybody there? Anybody there in the pub? My friend needs help!"

Some drunkards were roused in the pub, but they only heard muffled screams, which they couldn't make out. They shrugged their shoulders and continued drinking.

"This was not the way things should have ended," he spoke as tears dripped down on Brian's body. *"You didn't deserve this, brother. It's okay, you've stolen some goods, so what? It's no big deal ... Come on, come on now, open your eyes. I forgive you goddamn it, open your eyes!"*

Patrick hugged Brian and held him close to his heart. He didn't care for the blood smeared on his shirt. Patrick had never felt this kind of pain and sadness before. Brian was his friend, his brother, and his family. They both had a life ahead together, and they were to marry and go on so many voyages with the love of their lives. Tears raced down Patrick's eyes as his sobs got louder. It was as if a mountain of pain and sorrows had been dropped on Patrick's soul. He looked up to the sky and screamed in anguish and pain.

"NOOOO, oh, dear God noooo!!! Don't do this, please..." Patrick just sat there, screaming, crying, and

holding on to Brian's body even as it slid down from the blood's moisture. He felt devastated as a reel of memories with Brian passed by his eyes. An immense sadness had surrounded and settled in him after the loss of his best friend.

Patrick promised himself with a meek voice due to the desolation in his soul that he would avenge his friend's death. He would seek revenge on the people that had done this to his friend. A part of him did feel cheated by his best friend, but he also felt the guilt for changing the labels and being part of the cause of Brian's murder. He felt anger towards life, for not having enough time to make everything right.

After hearing the second screams, everybody in the pub streamed outside, feeling that someone needed their help. But it was too late. All they saw after they stepped outside were two best friends, both covered in blood. One lifeless and the other one mourning his death.

Chapter 17
A Heart-Rending Task

The next day, following his best friend's death, Patrick knew that he would have to be the one to break the awful news to Brian's father, Mr. Fuller. The thought of the loss made his heartache with grief. He had just lost his best friend, and the pain was agonizing. They had been together since forever and went through all kinds of experiences, including being in love.

Patrick couldn't even fathom what it would be like for Mr. Fuller to bear the news that Brian was never coming back. Even though he always acted harshly towards Brian, Patrick, and his deceased friend, both knew his father loved him at his core. No matter how much Patrick didn't want to be the messenger of bad news, he knew in his heart that it had to be him.

With a broken heart, Patrick walked into the kitchen of his house. His mother, Catherine, whom he had already given the news to, who had cried along with Patrick, immediately noticed the sadness in her son's bowed face and his swollen eyes. They had been crying all night for Brian, who was like a brother and son to them, respectively.

Catherine knew it was a difficult time for Patrick. No matter how strong and invincible she had raised him to be, the truth was that Patrick had a heart as soft as butter in the sun. It subdued just as easily as it melted – which she knew was the sign of a good heart. Grieving the loss of a dear friend and weighing its options of breaking the news to the friend's father. Catherine knew the conflict wasn't easy for her son. She also knew he would never back down from the colossal responsibility, so she wanted to help him.

"Patrick, would you rather have me announce the news to Mr. Fuller? I can do that for you, son."

"No, mother. I must do this myself. I owe it to Brian. I was ... I am his best friend," Patrick croaked.

He was on his way out the door when he stopped and looked back at his mom. His eyes looked heavy with the burden of his sadness and bewilderment. Catherine's eyes did not miss the silent cry in her son's imploring eyes. Without saying another word, she simply walked toward Patrick and took him into her arms. It was as if he was still a little boy, waiting to be comforted by her loving embrace. She wished she could take his pain away, but it was easier thought than done. Her own heart was in tatters, but no way near to Patrick's.

Catherine resorted to what she considered to be her stronghold – words. Still holding her son in an embrace, she began to speak, *"I know this is a difficult time, but this is what life is, and as hard as it is at times, you have to learn to accept it, son. Brian will live on, as long as you keep him dear to your heart."*

The expression on Patrick's face relaxed. A speck of gratitude glimmered in his eyes, and one final rivulet of tear trickled down. He knew he could always rely on his mother to say the right things at the right time, and he was thankful for it. To tell her that he understood what she said and that her lessons have always guided him through life, Patrick softly kissed his mother on the forehead and left. No words were spoken from Patrick, but they both knew that sometimes, words fell short for meaning. But the bond they shared, the silence, their mute actions, they were full of meaning.

Patrick was on his way to Mr. Fuller's house and with every step he got closer to the Fuller residence, his anxiety levels picked up a notch higher. He was quite nervous. The task at hand was a complex one. He had to tell an older man, his best friend's father, that his son was no more. It was tragic, but that didn't complicate matters as much as Patrick was never in Mr. Fuller's good books.

Greeting the man would be an ordeal in itself, let alone telling him that Brian was dead. Mr. Fuller never liked Patrick, and it had something to do with Brian showering more attention to his friend than his father, even living at his friend's house for some nights. Tricky thing – this jealousy – it brought out the worst in the best of people, thought Patrick.

He remembered Mr. Fuller was a joyful man, full of life and laughter when Patrick and Brian were little. But then the illness took Brian's mother. That's when everything changed – especially Mr. Fuller. He became the opposite of everything he was. He lost his appetite for love, life, and laughter. It seemed like the man who once spread happiness had nothing to do except make everybody around him feel miserable for no reason. It is strange how life can change a person, Patrick thought again. Strange how it molded people into taking one-eighty degree turns from who they were, what they like, and what makes them happy. At times, life is so cruel that it takes away everything we hold dear, like how it took Mr. Fuller's wife and, ultimately, now his son. One life left with no reason to live, fight, or even wake up in the morning. But human beings are remarkable creatures – they tend to find the will to slog on, even when life repeatedly knocks them to the ground. They find the will to survive – some with the positivity of Catherine, others with the crudeness of Mr. Fuller.

With so much racing through his mind, Patrick couldn't help but feel the despair he was going to let loose on Mr. Fuller. The old man had no idea his beloved son was already on the road to purgatory. Patrick quickly made a cross across his chest in the remembrance of his friend. The thoughts were driving him crazy. His steps became heavier with every passing second. He just wanted to get done with this ordeal … or maybe he didn't want to do it at all. Patrick couldn't make up his mind. He stopped mid-way and looked ahead of him. The wooden door was painted bright blue, with a frame so small that Brian's frame couldn't fit through it without ducking down a bit. The fond memory brought a smile to his face. *Was it okay to smile? Was he supposed to smile at the thought of his friend, who was now dead?* Patrick shoved the mangling thoughts aside, and like a man on a mission, marched to the blue door in front of him.

Once at Mr. Fuller's doorstep, Patrick calmed his mind down, took a couple of deep breaths, and mentally rehearsed how he was going to appraise the old man about the situation. His hand visibly shook as he raised it to knock the door, but he took a deep breath first, and then knocked on the painted blue wooden door. For a moment, there was complete silence inside. Patrick knocked again just to make sure Mr. Fuller heard it.

There was movement behind the door, a faint shuffle of steps drawing nearer, and then a cold voice answered, *"Who's there?"*

Patrick could hear the bitterness in Mr. Fuller's voice. Relaying the news was going to be more difficult than he had thought. Still determined to do what he came for, Patrick cleared up his throat and replied as clearly as his broken voice would allow him, *"It's me, Patrick."*

He could hear Mr. Fuller standing on the other side of the door, mumbling grumpily. If it were the good old days still, Patrick would have placed his bets on the mumbling being curses thrown at him by his friend's father. Even losing the bet would have been far better than the predicament he was in at the moment. His thoughts were interrupted by Mr. Fuller opening the door and his croaky voice again. He didn't seem too enthusiastic to have Patrick standing at his doorstep.

"Go away! Brian isn't home. He didn't even come home last night to sleep," Mr. Fuller said grumpily.

"I know Brian never came home last night Mr. Fuller, and that is exactly why I am here," Patrick gently replied.

"Whatever it is that you have to say, I am not interested. It couldn't be of much importance anyway. Just go away," Mr. Fuller seemed agitated and walked back inside, slamming the door.

Patrick shook his head with a mix of disbelief and despair. He never thought Mr. Fuller's dislike for him was so strong that he wouldn't even want to hear what he had to say. Patrick knocked on the door a second time. This time, he did it more convincingly.

"Mr. Fuller, you have to listen to me. There is a reason why Brian didn't come home last night ... something ... something happened to him," Patrick's voice pleaded Brian's father to believe him, and it looked like it worked.

There was a short silence before Mr. Fuller opened the door, squinted at him, and invited Patrick into the house. Patrick walked in without a word, his head hanging low. Mr. Fuller offered Patrick a chair to sit down before he made his stance clear.

"This better be serious because I don't have time to waste on stupidity," said the old man.

He really does not like me, Patrick thought. His mind wandered off once again. It kept going back to where Patrick wronged Mr. Fuller or when exactly. The truth was that none of it was Patrick's fault. Mr. Fuller had always been a family man. He saw his world in his wife and son. When his wife passed away, the man was broken, but at least he had his son – Brian. Since then, Brian became the center of his father's universe, but as the boy grew up, things changed. Brian and

Patrick had been inseparable since the beginning. With each passing year, their friendship grew better and stronger. They started working together, and that bridged all the gaps left in their bond. The more time the two friends spent together, the more neglected by his son Mr. Fuller felt, and his animosity towards Patrick grew. It was never Patrick's fault – at least that's what Patrick felt.

"You were saying?" Mr. Fuller's impatient voice brought Patrick back to reality.

Not sure where to start, Patrick took a moment to clear his head and recall all the ways he rehearsed breaking the news to this old man who made him extremely uncomfortable with his gaze. Patrick didn't know where to start.

"Speak up, young man. I hope this is not one of your stupid pranks?" the old man's restlessness was clear in every word he spoke.

"Mr. Fuller, there were certain things about Brian that you did not know about," Patrick began – starting from the beginning.

"What do you mean?" the old man retorted.

"What I mean is that Brian had been stealing from Miguel's stock to sell to the hoodlums. He was making extra money from it, and he got caught," Patrick explained.

For a split second, Mr. Fuller's eyes widened with comprehension, his pupils shuffled as they added things up, and then returned to normal. Patrick noticed that look on the old man's face. When Mr. Fuller heard everything Patrick told him about his son, he knew right away where all of Brian's money was coming from. Every single penny that Brian handed over to him wasn't hard-earned. It was stolen money, at least a good chunk of it.

Mr. Fuller was in a state of utter disbelief. He didn't know whether to laugh or cry, but he could feel a profound sense of guilt deep inside him. Patrick could read that in the way he swallowed the gulp in his throat. He realized that at some point, somehow, it was probably his fault that Brian got himself into all this nonsense. He looked at Patrick sitting in front of him and wondered whether he, too, was involved in the act and framed his son into getting caught. The boy had always been the smarter one of the two, and Mr. Fuller's cynical mind got the better of him, weaving one conspiracy theory after another over the gazillion possibilities involved. However, he kept all his thoughts to himself.

Without saying another word to Patrick or asking him what happened after his son got caught, Mr. Fuller quickly jumped to the conclusion that the crown had arrested Brian. If his son was in custody, it was his duty as a father to help him get out of there, or at least let him know that his father was on his side.

Mr. Fuller didn't wait for Patrick to finish his explanation. In his mind, there was no time to be wasted. They should be at the castle prison as soon as they can manage. The old man swiftly got up and put on his jacket. On his way rushing toward the door, he realized Patrick hadn't moved even an inch from his chair.

"Well, what are you waiting for? Let's go down to the quarters and help my little boy. He must be waiting for us. I am appalled that you didn't already take care of the matter. You'll have this old man walk up to the prison for something that could have been easily taken care of." Mr. Fuller addressed Patrick in his usual grumpy tone.

Patrick still didn't move. He remained seated, staring blankly at the desperate old man in front of him. He just nodded his head in the negative at Mr. Fuller, leaving the old man confused. He may have been old, but Mr. Fuller was no amateur. He could see the look on Patrick's face. The story Patrick started wasn't complete yet. There was more to it – something that was going to make this visit by Patrick a dreadful one. This story was certainly going to go from bad to worst. Mr. Fuller could sense it. The tension prevailing between the two men only made him more impatient. Worried that it might be too late if Patrick didn't speak up right away, Mr. Fuller walked up to him, grabbed him by the shoulder and shook him hard.

"Tell me you! Where is Brian? What happened to him? Where is my son?" he demanded, his voice loud and clear.

By now, the ache in Patrick's heart had turned into a tsunami of agony washing over his senses. He couldn't think straight, and he couldn't bring himself to tell Mr. Fuller the whole truth. His insides were crumbling down. Patrick could only imagine the pain this news would bring to this old man in front of him. Tell him to conquer the wildest of oceans, and Patrick wouldn't hesitate, but he was sure he never wanted to be in a situation like this. Patrick heaved a stuttering sigh, hoping it will take away the pain, but nothing changed. He then simply grabbed Mr. Fuller's arm, partly in hopes of seeking his undivided attention and partly to support his fragile frame, and then dropped the bomb.

"Mr. Fuller, your son is dead. Brian died last night. That's why he never came home," Patrick's flat voice delivered the message, and it felt like the ceiling would crumble at any moment.

For the first few seconds, Mr. Fuller did not believe what he had just heard. He simply studied Patrick's face, trying to locate any evidence that could prove otherwise. A prank, a disgusting prank. He wanted to grope at the hope of that, but no. He could see it in Patrick's eyes, all the pain and sorrow. The young man standing in front of him with a solemn expression on his face was not lying. It was, indeed, true. His son, his Brian, was no more.

Slowly the pain sank into his veins and bones. The arms Patrick held went limp as realization dawned on the old man in front of him. But it wasn't just grief that took over Mr. Fuller. There was more eating him up from the inside. It was the realization that his son was dead because of him. He was the cause of his son's death, and the pain of that realization surpassed anything that he had felt in ages. What made it worse was that his son was no longer there for him to ask forgiveness or be forgiven for all the ways he had wronged him. The pain inside of Mr. Fuller grew and grew until it morphed into a monster that fed on his anger and sorrow. He was desperate. There was so much he wanted to say to his son, so much to ask forgiveness for, so much to confess, and so much to share, but Brian would never give him the chance to make up for all that – not now, not ever.

His eyes brimmed with unshed tears as he looked at Patrick. He wanted to partially blame it on the young man standing in front of him. Patrick was Brian's best friend; he should have protected him. There was more anger inside him, but Mr. Fuller knew in his heart that no matter how much he disliked Patrick, the boy would never harm his son. It had to be someone else. *Who was responsible?*

"Who did it?" he asked Patrick, still trying to sound sharp. *"I want names. Who did this? Who was responsible for my boy's death? I need to go after them,"* his temper rising, Mr. Fuller was shaking with a deadly combination of anger, pain, and sorrow.

Patrick took hold of Mr. Fuller and sat him down.

"You need to calm down, Mr. Fuller. This wrath isn't going to help you get anywhere."

The boy made sense; Mr. Fuller realized. He took a deep breath and tried to control the tempest inside of him. However, even as he reasonably analyzed the whole situation, he found himself face to face with the person holding the entire guilt for this episode of his life – it was him – Mr. Fuller, himself.

"I loved my son. I always loved him. I know I was never able to show it, but I always cared about him. He was my son, my boy," Mr. Fuller was looking at Patrick as words flooded out of his mouth, a mixture of despair and despondency.

He wanted Patrick to believe him. Mr. Fuller tried to change the situation somehow, but the pain within him just inflated to the point where he couldn't take it anymore. All the emotions he felt – the grief, the pain, the anger, the frustration – exploded together to mourn his loss. Mr. Fuller burst into tears, sobbing hysterically as Patrick stood there, holding him by his arms.

Patrick didn't know how long he stood there. He had no words to comfort a man who would have to live with the sorrow of losing his only son for the rest of his life. The best he could do was to be there for the old man, and that's what he did. He stayed there with Mr. Fuller as his hysterical sobs subdued into a perennial stream of tears flowing from his eyes, and then eventually hiccups followed by sniffles.

Once the tears dried, Patrick knew he needed to give Mr. Fuller some time to mourn in solitude. With the resolve to keep a regular check on the old man, Patrick silently left Mr. Fuller and his house to head back home.

Chapter 18
Unexpected Loss

Patrick had never imagined that his dearest friend and companion would die in front of his eyes. He never even came close to thinking that Brian would take his last breath in his arms. They both had so much left to do together. They had always wanted to sail somewhere other than the Mediterranean Sea, and drink foreign wines and meet emphatic rulers and traders.

They wanted to try their luck by taking their trade goods to another country and set up shop for a couple of weeks just for the sake of having that unique experience. Both had agreed that it would be a great and exciting adventure.

A few days went by after Brian's funeral, and Patrick was still trying to come to terms with Brian's death. He knew he had a responsibility to get back to his ship, but he had a very good reason not to be there. The guilt was heavy, and Patrick felt he had played a big role in Brian's demise. Patrick's crew knew that he was going through a rough time in mourning Brian's death and didn't expect him to be okay anytime soon. But they really wanted their captain back. They had not sailed since Brian's passing. The ship was gathering dust as if it hadn't moved from the docks for ages. That morning, Miguel came on board with a glum look on his face.

He gathered the crew at the dock and stood before them.

Miguel said, *"This is a very tough time for us all. Brian was an important member of our group as well as for the brotherhood we shared together. He will be dearly missed."*

He went silent for a bit and then continued, *"It's going to be a lot more difficult for Patrick. Brian's loss would take a bit of time for him to sail again since they were the best of friends. But y'all don't need to worry because I am doing the best I can to get Patrick back to his ship and back at sea. The sooner, the better, Iy? But in the meantime, I'll be taking over the ship,"* he said, and with that, their meeting came to an end.

The new captain ordered the crew to get back to their duties and prepared the ship for travel. The crew immediately dispersed to their chores and prepared for the trip. They were already a couple of days late with a delivery, and Miguel had to get things back on track, and that too within a very short period of time. The crew had to work with their boss, which gave them an even better reason to want Patrick back as their captain as soon as possible. They lined the goods that needed to be loaded and made all the necessary arrangements that needed to be made before they sailed. Once the ship was loaded, off they went. Their first stop was Tangier.

As per their routine, they anchored at the docks of Tangier, and the crewmen unloaded the cargo. Miguel had already done this before, so he knew the drill. He was aware of what needed to be done and how things were to go from then on. He got off the ship and made his way through the docks and walked towards the city. Miguel stopped in front of the first store of the marketplace and took out a bell from a pouch he was carrying.

It was the middle of the day, so the market was bustling with a highly active crowd. All Miguel could see was bobbing heads to as far as his eyes could see. Tangier's marketplace was one of the busiest places in the city, and Miguel knew that. He had stopped there simply to announce their arrival. Miguel had a very old-school way of doing things. He thought the old-school ways were more effective, and contrary to what the youth would think, they worked all the time. That's why he had brought his bell with him. While going through the marketplace, Miguel would ring his bell while loudly announcing to everyone that they were in the port, ready to sell some goods and make some money. At the same time, Miguel would also announce to the merchants that their ordered merchandise had arrived. The sound of the bell was heard far and wide.

Ahmed and Sabah were in their shop. They were busy arranging their merchandise neatly on their shelves when they heard the familiar sound. They looked at each other and concluded it could only be one person. Upon hearing the announcement, they were startled and surprised. Although their shipment was late, which had never happened in many years of service, this wasn't important at the moment.

What really took them by surprise was hearing someone else's voice making the announcement. Ahmed's old memories were stimulated by hearing the sound of the bell. They were used to Brian announcing the arrival of their trade goods, but this was definitely not the voice they were hearing. Ahmed didn't really know what to think or say at this particular time. He looked at Sabah's face. She was concerned and sensed a bad omen. Ahmed thought he should find out what was going on. He opened the door and walked outside while Sabah stayed in the doorway with bated breath. She watched her father make his way through the crowd, following the sound of the bell.

As Ahmed got closer to the pealing sound, he recognized the voice making the announcement; it was Miguel. Both Ahmed and Miguel knew each other very well. Miguel had overseen this task many years ago, long before Brian and Patrick had started delivering their merchandise. Ahmed ran towards Miguel and thought he would poke a little fun with him. He went close to him from the back and tipped Miguel's cap over from his head. The cap fell in front of his eyes.

Miguel stopped shouting and was startled. He placed his cap back on his head and turned around. As soon as he saw Ahmed, a big smile spread across his face. They hadn't seen each other for years. Instantly, they pulled each other into an embrace like long lost friends. Miguel took a few minutes from his duties to talk to Ahmed, but he had limited time. There were a lot of things that he had to take care of. The shipments were already days late, and Miguel had no time to lose. Ahmed had a lot of questions for Miguel and was also very persistent that he stops by the store to have a cup of coffee.

Miguel didn't really have any time to spare, but replied, *"Ahmed, no worries laddy, I will try my best to stop by,"* He didn't want to upset Ahmed by flatly refusing his invitation.

He was so happy to see Miguel that Ahmed completely forgot to ask about the boys and how they were doing. Remembering it on his way back to his store, he turned around and ran back to Miguel.

Catching up with him, Ahmed asked Miguel, *"Hey Miguel, where are the boys? I don't see them today. Did they take some time off?"*

Miguel was flustered for a second, but he tried to recover immediately. *"Oh yeah ... e-everything is fine. There is no need to worry. P-Patrick will be back next week."*

Ahmed, sensitive to Miguel's tone of voice picked up a strange sense of uncertainty in Miguel's voice and noted that he didn't mention anything about Brian.

Ahmed, concerned with his daughter's interest, continued, *"And how about Brian? He will certainly be back with Patrick, right? Or maybe you made him the captain of his own ship?"* Ahmed added with a little chuckle and a little slap over his friend's shoulder.

Miguel dreaded the question. He continued to walk forward as if he had not heard it. Ahmed did not like this little game. He knew something wasn't right. He grabbed Miguel by the arm and turned him around to face him.

He said, *"Okay, Miguel, cut it out. I am not a child. Tell me what's going on with the boys? Is something wrong?"*

Miguel nodded his head and said, *"I can't, Ahmed. I just can't."*

Ahmed felt frustrated.

"Well if you can't," Ahmed disappointed, *"there must be someone else who can answer my question. Who can I speak to that will tell me what's going on? Oh! Yes, your crew. They know me very well, maybe they have something to say."*

Miguel grabbed Ahmed by the arm as he turned around to head for the ship, waited a moment, looked into Ahmed's eyes, then took off his cap and unwillingly agreed to talk about Brian.

"I wish I had not been the chosen one to talk about this to you because I, like everyone else, know that Brian and Sabah were in love," he started talking.

Miguel recounted the whole story to Ahmed but decided to omit the detail that Brian had passed away. He couldn't bring himself to reveal that Ahmed just yet. He would crumble, and Miguel couldn't be the one to break his friend like that.

Ahmed looked at Miguel and said to him with raised eyebrows, *"So the boy got in a little bit of trouble, huh? Was that really so hard to explain?"* He was about to let out a sigh of relief, but then Ahmed recalled the way Miguel announced how Brian and Sabah *"were"* in love. The past tense stuck in Ahmed's throat like a thorn. He asked Miguel about it again but more specifically why did Miguel use this choice of word.

Miguel stayed quiet and closed his eyes. He didn't want to say it, but he had no choice.

"What I am about to tell you friend, is the most difficult thing that I have had to do in a long time. But I won't spin this in circles anymore. Here is the truth, Brian is dead. He

died by a beating he got from the hoodlums. Patrick was the one who changed the labels on the boxes. Because of this circumstance, Brian delivered the wrong merchandise to the hoodlums. Patrick had changed the labels on the boxes to find out who the thief was and did so without telling anyone about it. Patrick had no idea Brian was the thief, he of all people. But the hoodlums learned about it and ... "

Ahmed couldn't take it anymore. He bent down and grabbed his knees. All he could do was say the words, *"Oh My God, this cannot be true."* The news caught him by the most shocking of surprises. He was shattered and couldn't stop thinking about Sabah. The turn of events was so unexpected he didn't know what to say or do. Miguel apologized to Ahmed and excused himself because he really had to get back to the ship. Ahmed replied in a flat tone, *"I understand, friend."*

Before leaving, he turned around and said to Ahmed, *"I know this isn't fair, the pain of this event is driving us all mad, but now that you know, you really need to be the one to tell your daughter. She needs to know and from you only. You will be able to handle it well and take care of her. This is going to hurt, and she'll need you more than anything."*

Miguel's parting words made Ahmed only feel worse.

He walked back to the store, and all he could think about was how on earth was he going to explain this tragedy to his daughter. She loved Brian with all her heart and soul. He knew the news would crush her.

Sabah was standing at the door, reading her father's face closely. She had been standing there, waiting for an explanation about Brian's absence. Ahmed looked at her face and could see she had been worried sick ever since he had stepped out of the shop. She must have thought of all the worst-case scenarios during the time he was away. Could she have thought about his death, he wondered. Wouldn't her consideration make it easier for him? She would come to expect it. Thus, it wouldn't be so hard, would it?

Ahmed, extremely confused, still didn't want to tell her, not yet at least. He took a deep breath and holding back with all his strength, said to Sabah, *"It was Miguel. There is nothing to worry about, dear. The boys took some time off. They will be back soon."*

He didn't know if Sabah actually believed what he had told her, but he was not ready to give an explanation to her and break her heart. All he focused on was the relief he felt when he saw Sabah close her eyes, take a breath, and smile. She seemed happy as if there was nothing wrong. Miguel predicted that she hadn't expected the worst news she could possibly hear, and she was definitely not ready to hear it just yet. Not from him, not today at least.

Ahmed then asked Sabah to go home and help her mother.

"I will see you at dinner. Don't worry about the shop. I will manage it." He said that convincingly, but the truth was, he didn't want anyone close to the store to talk to Sabah about Brian before he could tell her about this awful news himself. That kind of news usually spreads around like wildfire.

The entire day went by, and all Ahmed was thinking were thoughts about how to break the news to Sabah. He hadn't paid any attention to the customers that had walked into his shop all day. He didn't remember what items he sold today, and whether he had quoted the right prices for each of the purchased articles.

There was nothing he could think about, but Sabah. At twilight, he closed his shop and made his way home. Ahmed arrived home, and as usual, his supper was ready. Sabah greeted him cheerfully, and he replied, trying to form a smile. He washed his hands and proceeded to the kitchen table. Ahmed was still not ready to explain to Sabah what had happened, but he knew that he had to find the courage to say it. The longer he would keep it from her, the worse it would make it for both of them.

They, Ahmed, Sabah, and her mother, sat down at the table, and it was noticeably quiet. A little too quiet than usual. Just to start a conversation and lighten the mood, Sabah asked her father if he was tired today.

Ahmed looked up and said, *"Yes, dear. There were a lot of customers today, so yes, I am feeling a bit tired ... and that's probably the reason why I'm not saying much."*

Unable to get the conversation going, Sabah proceeded to ask a second question.

She asked her father, *"Have you placed an order for items that we need from Gibraltar? We are running low on stock."*

Ahmed knew that Sabah was asking that question because she thought about possibly seeing Brian next week. Now was probably a good time to reveal the bad news.

Without answering his daughter's question, Ahmed looked at his daughter and wife and began by telling them that there had been a tragedy. He looked at his daughter and said, *"Please forgive me, daughter, for not telling you about it earlier. I should have told you about it this morning, but I was trying to protect you and could not find the words to explain what had happened. I guess I needed some time ..."*

Sabah, not feeling very well, asked her father, in a forgiving way, to deliver this news. *"Please Papa, I am not a child anymore."* Sabah was back to the feelings she had that same morning when Brian was absent from his normal duties.

Ahmed continued explaining what had happened to Brian in Gibraltar, but without mentioning that Brian was dead. Sabah put her hand on her heart and felt anxious. Knowing that her love was a secret, she kept all her feelings and emotions to herself. Ahmed described how the hoodlums had beaten him up. Again, he did not mention anything about Brian's demise, but he knew that Sabah wasn't too well bearing the news of her lover's beating. As Ahmed reached the end of his explanation, he told himself that he had come this far, and he had to break the final barrier. He looked at his daughter and said, *"Sabah, you will always be my little child regardless of how old you might be, and I would never dream of hurting you in any way. But this will hurt you and I am so sorry for being the person to deliver this news to you... Brian couldn't recover from his injuries."*

Instantly, the remaining color on Sabah's face drained in just a few seconds.

Ahmed looked at Sabah while swallowing the lump in his throat and said, *"Sabah, Brian is no more. He has left us. He is never coming back to Tangier."*

Sabah's heart shattered to pieces. She was suddenly overwhelmed with grief and sorrow. It was as if her whole being had been thrown off a cliff. Ahmed saw the tears building up in Sabah's eyes, his daughter was in shock. She was still canning her emotions out of respect for her culture. Ahmed stood up and went to sit beside her.

He took her hand and said to her, *"I can only wish that you meet a man someday who can put so much love into your heart as Brian did."*

Sabah's lip quivered, as she leaped on and embraced her father in tears. She held him as tightly as she could. At that point, it was just too overwhelming. She could not hold her emotions back any longer, regardless of everything she had been taught about her culture. She had lost the love of her life, and she was hurt beyond repair as she felt her whole body being torn apart, her heart imploding, and her life that once had significance, become meaningless.

Chapter 19
Unforeseen Providence

Back at Layla's palace, life was miraculously much better. Layla had offered Moustapha a room after he had tended to Samira. She offered him food and shelter as a show of gratitude and told him that he could stay for as long as he wanted.

Moustapha resisted at first, but then reluctantly accepted her hospitality. *"Thank you so much, but I will only be staying until Samira has fully recovered,"* he told her with a smile. Moustapha was pleased to have a place to stay in Fez. He wanted to stay away from the marketplace for a little while and get some rest.

A month went by, and Samira completely recovered from her illness. Moustapha was immensely proud and satisfied with Samira's convalescence. However, he also felt that it was time for him to leave. Moustapha was fully rested, and gathered Layla and Fatima to announce his departure, *"I am incredibly grateful for the hospitality you have shown me, but it is time. I must move on and do what I do best, help people, and many need me back home, wherever that may be,"* he told Layla and Fatima. *"I would like to ask for a favor before I leave. Could I have you transport me to Tangier? I have close family there and I haven't seen them for a very long time.* he said with a dishonorable look.

Layla obliged Moustapha's request, asking Mohammed to prepare two horses and a carriage for him. She also requested that Fatima accompany him on the trip so she could assist Moustapha and make his long journey to Tangier more comfortable. During this time, Hanane would have to stay home to look after the children and chores.

Fatima agreed to go. Mohammed loaded all the necessities for the trip onto the carriage, and they got ready for their journey to Tangier.

The following day, at Tangier's port, Patrick's ship had arrived and docked at the harbor. It was carrying a special delivery.

Miguel had deemed Patrick fit to get back on his ship because he didn't want his navigating and sailing abilities to rust away because of Brian's passing. Ever since the funeral, Patrick had decided to stay home, in his room, filled with guilt. He hadn't found the strength to absolve himself for what he had done. Thanks to Miguel's persistence, he had no choice but to get back to his ship. Miguel was convinced that staying at home mourning Brian's death and continuously revisiting all the bad decisions he might have taken was definitely unhealthy for the young lad. He was already in pretty rough shape when he had found out that Brian was the one stealing cargo off the ship. The feelings of deceit and betrayal had disturbed him, and Patrick had been finding it hard to shake them off.

Furthermore, Patrick did sit in a puddle of Brian's blood while forgiving him and holding him in his arms as he breathed his last breath. He couldn't save his best friend's life. It was the most terrifying moment of his life, and he wouldn't wish it on his worst enemy.

Patrick went back to navigating his ship as per Miguel's recommendation. Catherine also agreed that this was the best course of action for her son. But was it really?

Patrick began taking long journeys and trade routes. He was working harder than ever to escape the void of a best friend. As time went by, Patrick grew weaker and lost a substantial amount of weight. He wasn't eating correctly and would work endlessly until someone told him to stop and take a break. For several weeks, he worked consistently, taking small breaks in-between. Patrick had lost his way and wasn't able to focus on the life he previously enjoyed. There was no hope, there was no faith, Brian was gone, and he was never coming back.

Today the ship docked in Tangier, the crew unloaded the ship as usual. Patrick decided it was time for him to pay a visit to Ahmed and Sabah. He didn't see anyone since Brian's death; he just hadn't felt up to it. But now, he was concerned about their wellbeing. It was high time they were told about Brian and his untimely death, he thought.

Patrick walked off the ship and strolled along the docks. Since no one was expecting his ship to arrive at Tangier, he didn't think much about the lack of traders. Slightly disheartened, Patrick returned to the ship and gave his crew the rest of the day off. *"Go to the city and have fun. I'll stay on the ship and enjoy this beautiful evening's hospitality,"* he told them. As soon as everyone left the ship, Patrick went into his cabin to rest for a while. He told himself that he would visit Ahmed and Sabah later.

Mohammed arrived, the following day, at the marketplace in Tangier which was around the same time Patrick's ship had docked in the port. Moustapha stepped out of the carriage and picked up his belongings. He was utterly grateful to have Fatima, who entertained him throughout the journey to Tangier.

Fatima was incredibly grateful to him and stepped out of the carriage and said, *"Thank you so much, Moustapha. I hope I will see you again someday. You can come and visit us anytime you wish. You have been incredibly helpful to our family, and in the process, you became part of our family as well. You are not a stranger to us anymore."* Moustapha was pleased about the way things turned out between him, Fatima, and her family. He thanked Fatima dearly and said farewell. It was time for him to move on with his life and continue searching for someone else who might require his help.

Fatima suddenly realized she was back in Tangier. She had many fond memories associated with this city, especially ones that she held dear to her heart, Sabah, Patrick, Brian, the dance, the stagecoach plan. She decided to relive some of those memories and walked to the cliff all by herself. She wanted to be alone and feel that familiar feeling of the cool wind of the sea wrapped around her. Since Samira was cured and wasn't a priority anymore, she had this strange sense of melancholia and longing for Patrick to come back to the surface. She wanted to walk those feelings off and turn them into something that resembled love and belonging. This cliff was where she saw Patrick for the first time after they'd met, so the cliff held great importance for her and their spiritual bond.

Fatima was determined to wait for Patrick for as long as she could, even if it meant a lifetime. Yet, that didn't stop her from being a little impatient regarding her situation from time to time.

Life hadn't exactly made it easy for them to see each other again after their first touch, but she knew in her heart that it would happen again someday. She went up to the cliff, closed her eyes, and released all the energy that was buried in her just to get through the sad reality of life. Once it was gone, she could regenerate the thoughts of love again. As she opened her eyes at the top of the cliff, she gazed towards the port.

A surprise crept up her spine. She wasn't sure what she saw, so she ran a bit higher to confirm if she had seen correctly, or if she was simply out of her mind.

Fatima's heart started to pound so loudly she feared it would rip right out of her chest. Her body charged up as she reached out with one hand to touch the far-out ship that belonged to the man she loved so much. She brought her other hand towards her mouth, and tears ran down from her cheeks, leaving a trace of euphoria. At that particular moment in time, she knelt on the ground and thanked God for timing this right.

As Fatima squinted and stared at the ship, she realized there was no one aboard the ship or even around it. A powerful sense of curiosity surged within her. Fatima stood up and started to descend the cliff heading towards the ship. She got closer, engulfed by nervousness, and kept walking towards the ship. A

voice whispered in her ear that it was all right to continue. She braced herself and walked up the ship's plank and made it onto the main deck. It was at that moment when Fatima became extremely nervous. She didn't think it was such a good idea anymore. She turned around to get back onto the ship's plank and off the ship as soon as she could, but then she paused. She had heard someone cough, and she was sure the sound came from the captain's cabin. Even though her heart was racing, and she had never been so nervous and out of place, she couldn't walk away. She had to turn around and meet the love of her life. At least that's who she hoped it was. If that was to be true, she was on the ship alone with no one on board except Patrick. What a clear sign of fate that would be and just like her dream had shown her, she thought.

Fatima walked towards the captain's cabin, and with each footstep she took, her heartbeat would speed up a little more. As she arrived at the door, she lifted the latch and walked right into the room.

She closed the door, the latch locked, and the bit of noise it made awakened Patrick. He turned around with a drowsy look on his face. He thought that Knot had just entered the room, but from where he was, in bed, he couldn't see the door. He assumed it was Knots because there was no reply when he asked, *"Who is it?"* Patrick put his head back on his pillows. *"You should be with the others having fun. Remember Knot never be afraid to make new friends,"* he said, intoxicated with sleep. Just hearing the sound of his voice made Fatima freeze where she stood. Her back stood straight against the door; her eyes closed as she lifted her head toward the ceiling. When Patrick noticed that he wasn't getting any response from whomever it was that had entered the room, he sat up in his bed. Wiping his eyes, he was getting ready to see who entered the room. At that same instant, Fatima decided to bring herself into the dim light, face to face with the man she loved. Patrick lifted his head and didn't fully believe what his eyes were looking at. He went about, wiping his eyes, and looked up again. Nothing had changed. Thinking it was all a dream, he was staring directly at the woman he loved – Fatima.

She was still the most beautiful woman he had ever seen. Patrick smiled, and his heart began to beat harder. Patrick stood up and ambled towards her not to scare her off, thinking this might still be a dream. He came to a halt only a few inches from her heart. He could feel the resonance of her heart intertwine while being rhythmic to his own. The strong beat of his heart led to a soft touch of her hand as he realized it was no longer a dream. Overwhelmed, Patrick fell to his knees and wrapped his arms around her legs, hugging them strongly to express how happy he was to see her. After all the unfortunate events, Patrick was finally compensated with an ecstatic reunion. Fatima replied to the gesture by moving her arm forward, caressing his hair with her hand, breaking into a poignant chuckle. Without a doubt, this was nothing less than true love, and nothing felt better to them than being together. Fatima bent over and took Patrick's hands to help him up. Even before Patrick could stand on his own feet, she pulled the man that she loved into her arms and embraced him. They were overwhelmed with happiness, love, and emotion as they quickly collided in a passionate kiss.

Their bodies entwined with each other like tight threaded rope holding sails on a ship. Fatima had waited an exceptionally long time for this moment, and there was no stopping her from showing her love. Emotions of affection flooded the room, which led to another kiss. To feel their lips against each other's was something they both had dreamed about for so long. After the kiss, they held each other close and looked at one another, panting with desire. The sorrow of being away from each other for so long faded with each kiss. Unexpectedly, while Patrick was taking a deep breath, he moved away from Fatima with an odd look on his face.

Fatima immediately understood that there was something wrong. She looked at Patrick, gasping for air. In a matter of seconds, he fell to the floor with a light sheen of sweat that washed all over his face. Fatima was utterly stunned and went into a little state of panic. She knelt beside him and touched his forehead with her palm. She recognized that it was due to some illness and knew it wasn't good.

Fatima stood up and ran out of Patrick's cabin with a hand bowl she had found in his room. She filled the container with water from a barrel and ran back to him. She couldn't find any loose piece of cloth with which she could dab Patrick's face. She ripped a thick strip of her dress, soaked it with water, and wiped the sweat off his face. She thought it would help bring down his high body temperature, but it wasn't enough.

Fatima knew she had to get help. She soaked the ripped piece of cloth in the water for one last time and placed it on Patrick's forehead before running out of the room and off the ship to call for help. She ran towards Ahmed's shop and prayed dearly with her heart to find someone who could help her. Ahmed had just arrived at his merchant's shop, accompanied by Sabah. While he was unpacking, he heard someone calling his name out loud. He turned around to see who it was. *"My God,"* he said to himself as he saw Fatima running towards him, shocked and clearly troubled. Fatima was sobbing, and all she could manage to say was *"Ahmed, Patrick, Ahmed,"* while pointing towards the shipyard. Ahmed tried to calm her down so she could catch her breath, but he also noticed that her dress was torn.

His mind immediately jumped to the worst conclusion possible. He didn't know what was going on and was quite confused, but he knew Patrick wouldn't harm Fatima. That was not possible. Finally, Fatima calmed down enough to speak. *"Patrick is terribly ill. He is lying down on the floor of his cabin on the ship. Please come and have a look at him,"* she explained to Ahmed.

Without knowing what was wrong with Patrick, Ahmed called out to Sabah telling her to bring freshwater and the first aid kit they kept in the shop. Sabah was just as confused upon receiving this order, so she ran out of the store with the water and first aid kit to see what was going on. When she saw her father and Fatima in a state of terror walking towards the port, she didn't know what to think. If her father was worried, something very wrong had happened. Sabah ran fast enough to catch up to them. On their way to the ship, Sabah learned about the whole story. Ahmed dashed into the captain's cabin to find Patrick lying on the floor, still clinging onto life. Ahmed kneeled down beside him to examine him and realized that Patrick was barely breathing. He looked up at Fatima with death written all over his face. Fatima looked puzzled. She had recognized Patrick's condition, and it was the same as Samira's illness. Knowing the illness, Fatima was convinced that Patrick must have had it for a while, but she didn't share her thoughts.

Ahmed was no doctor and he had no clue what to do. He just knew one thing; he couldn't give up on him. He started thinking out loud and thought he'd probably need a miracle to get Patrick out of this predicament. As he lifted Patrick to his bed, all he could think of was to pray they could get a doctor here on time.

Fatima was stunned by this event and Sabah suddenly realized, "How is Fatima even here?". She asked Fatima, how did you get to Tangier. Fatima, who cannot see anything beyond Patrick, continued to whisper a name to herself. Her voice grew louder and louder as she chanted, *"Moustapha, Moustapha, Moustapha"* repeatedly.

Ahmed knew of Moustapha and his healings. He turned around and proclaimed that he would need another miracle to get Moustapha here on time. Fatima explained that she had accompanied Moustapha to Tangier before coming to the port. Ahmed didn't quite understand why she had accompanied Moustapha to Tangier, but that story would have to wait.

Upon learning this new information, Ahmed looked at Fatima and Sabah and instructed them to find Moustapha as fast as they could. The two girls ran back to the marketplace as fast as they could to find Moustapha. Luckily, Fatima found him not too far from where she had dropped him off. She was still in a state of panic but tried to give a brief explanation to Moustapha about the whole situation.

Now that Moustapha knew what the urgency was, everyone was in a hurry to get back to the ship. A concerned merchant that overheard the conversation offered them a fast ride back with his horse-drawn carriage. They got into the carriage and quickly reached the port. The minute Moustapha looked at Patrick, he looked up at Fatima to tell her that the man is an infidel. Before Fatima could open her mouth to reply, Ahmed said to Moustapha, *"If you do not save this man, God could take all of our lives and bring us down to hell. This man may be an outsider by birth, but his heart is one of ours, and that is the reason why we call him 'Mehdi.' That means rightly guided, the bringer of good."*

Ahmed was overly concerned about Patrick's condition; he should have been tended to much sooner. Moustapha stood where he was for a moment, then took a step forward to examine Patrick's condition. Ahmed, with great sorrow, grabbed Moustapha's arm and confirmed, *"He is like a son to me, and he's extremely good to our people. Saving this young man's life is something you must do!"* Moustapha thought for a moment and asked everybody to clear the captain's cabin.

Everyone moved out and gathered onto the ship's deck. The last person that came out of the cabin closed the door behind. Love had brought them together after life had split them apart. Destiny was at work, and it would have to be seen if their fate would be dominated by either love or by the cruel ways of life. Fatima was worried about Patrick, but she had to leave the same day due to her obligations. They were not married, which made it very complicated for Fatima to decide to stay by his side again due to her cultural differences. She had made Sabah promise to look after him in her absence. *"I will come back as soon as possible,"* Fatima told her.

Patrick had managed to hold on long enough for Moustapha to nurse him back to life despite his frail condition. Sabah stayed by Patrick's side to look after him, as she had promised Fatima. Ahmed made sure to send the news to Miguel, informing him about what had happened.

As soon as Miguel got the news, he set sail to Tangier to pick up Patrick and Moustapha. When he brought Patrick home, Catherine was distraught to see her son in such a condition. Catherine was so shaken up that she could not even imagine what her son was going through. Moustapha was dearly compensated with Catherine's hospitality until Patrick fully recovered.

A couple of weeks later, Patrick was back on his feet and back as the captain of his ship. This little episode had knocked a lot of sense into him and helped him realize it was good to be alive. Patrick just had to accept the past how it was for the basic reason that there's nothing anyone could ever do to change it.

Fatima was indeed a really good reason for Patrick to be alive and every day he was at home healing; his mind would bring him back to this memorable moment in time. Remembering his pleasant encounter with Fatima in his quarters, on his ship. Fatima most definitely had to be part of his life and he needed to make this wrong side of life right, at all cost. But little did he know that he would be the one to take this right, away from himself.

Patrick woke up this very sunny morning planning to bring Moustapha back to Tangier. But Catherine, a bit headstrong about her son's health, decided to let him rest and had already brought Moustapha back to Miguel's docks. There Miguel had voluntarily brought Moustapha back to Tangier, where he would get back to his daily life as a vagabond seeking to help others with his gift of healing.

Chapter 20
The Opportunity of a
Lifetime!?

A few days after Moustapha was taken back to Tangier, Miguel, in Gibraltar, had received a letter from his brother-in-law requesting a favor. His brother-in-law had a dear friend living somewhere near the shores of the Caribbean Sea, who needed trade goods to be shipped to "The Settlement" in the Virgin Islands. The British Virgin Islands, situated in the Caribbean Sea, had been captured by the Brits in 1648.

Once the trade goods were delivered to The Settlement, sugarcane was to be loaded onto the ship at no extra cost, and it would be up to Miguel to commence the trade routes for sugarcane in Europe and Africa. It was the perfect opportunity for Miguel to broaden his horizons and step outside of his comfort zone. He had never sailed nor sent his freight through the Caribbean, and this was an excellent occasion to embark on this journey. Miguel gladly accepted the contract, especially knowing that the shipment would make him a lot of money. It was going to be far more interesting than local trades too, he thought. Miguel assembled an experienced crew, hired a highly recommended captain with combat experience, and prepared his biggest ship, The Maiden of the Sea, for the journey. Once the ship was ready to sail, Miguel christened the voyage by breaking a champagne bottle, Laurent-Perrier, at the front of the ship. Little did people know; Miguel would have never wasted a good bottle of champagne on a ship; that was plain sinful and immoral to his beliefs.

The night before, he had transferred the contents and filled the bottle with carbonated water. Carbonated water was a new invention at the time but very useful to Miguel for saving a great bottle of champagne. Off went the blessed ship climbing up to new horizons ahead. *"May the Maiden of the Sea quiver the ocean until she lands into the Caribbean Sea,"* Miguel cried with glee from the docks while his sailors cheered. A few weeks passed, and Miguel didn't hear from his vessel or its crew. With each passing day, he worried a bit more. He received no news from the captain he hired, no note, no letter, and to make matters worse; a rumor spread far and wide that a pirate named

Blackbeard was at large again and extremely active. Miguel had learned that Blackbeard looted every ship that came his way. People alleged that the pirate took everything he could get his hands on, without a care for the law or the people he pillaged. His conquest of the Caribbean Sea was expected to be only a matter of time.

Miguel ran down to the port to find Patrick and explained the entire situation to him. Patrick was surprised when he heard about Blackbeard. He had always thought the infamous pirate was a myth, a tale people told to amuse themselves. Patrick was the best navigator Miguel had in his fleet, and being paranoid with disconcertment, he offered Patrick an opportunity.

The opportunity consisted of voyaging across the Atlantic Ocean, using the same route the Maiden of the Sea would have taken, and that to ensure the Maiden of the Sea made it safely through to the Caribbean Sea. He would also be transporting the same trade goods in case the Maiden of the Sea did not make it. This calling also meant Patrick was granted Miguel's fastest ship, The Black Marlin. The Black Marlin was similar to the Maiden of the Sea, but had no defense system onboard, which made it substantially lighter and extremely faster. Patrick was ecstatic and could not believe his ears. He was just offered the opportunity to an adventure of a lifetime. One he could never imagine happening anytime soon. He was about to embark on his dream voyage, navigating the Black Marlin at incredible speeds. Out of excitement, Patrick grabbed Miguel very quickly by his sideburns, pulled his face towards his own, puckered up, and smacked his lips. *"Prepare yer ship matey, we're sailing to the Caribbean arrgh!"* he said with a grin. He then ran to the stable, got onto his horse, and fled home to share his excitement with his Mom.

Patrick arrived home, jumped off his horse, and yelled, *"Mom, I'm home. Where are you?"* He was anxious to tell his mother about this exciting opportunity. Patrick found her in the kitchen where she was busy preparing dinner. All riled up by his exhilaration, he told his Mom about Miguel's offer, almost using just one single breath. His mother was stunned upon hearing the news. Catherine was not in agreement with Miguel's proposition but managed to hold back her emotions because she didn't want to disappoint. Patrick's health had just gotten better after the difficult time he had mourning Brian's death. This opportunity was one that made him very happy, and his mom was not going to spoil it. She hugged and congratulated her son, saying, *"I am so proud of you, my son. May God bless you with more success, Amen."* She prayed for him and kissed him on his forehead.

After that, it was time for her to go. Catherine quickly picked up her bag and told Patrick that she had to run an errand. She stepped out before Patrick could ask where she was going. Patrick felt a bit strange about her reaction but didn't make anything of it. He was mostly preoccupied with the thoughts of the journey that lied ahead.

The smile on Catherine's face vanished as soon as she got out of the house. She had in her mind to meet Miguel with no intention of being kind to the man. She was furious at his readiness to push her son into the face of danger. Everyone knew that Blackbeard was dangerous and navigated the Caribbean Sea; his lust for blood and wealth were second to none.

The Queen of England was also offering a very generous bounty to anyone who would capture Blackbeard and bring him to the lawful authorities. Catherine was aware of Miguel's little habits after work and knew precisely where to find him – the Green Sail Pub.

Upon reaching the pub, Catherine stormed in through the door, looked around, and at once saw her target. Miguel was laughing and drinking with some of his friends.

Joy washed away from Miguel's face and replaced with guilt when he noticed Catherine coming towards him with a grave expression on her face. Not knowing what to do, he quickly rose from his chair and tried to sneak outside.

Not only his circle of friends but everyone who he passed grew baffled by the sudden change in his demeanor. Also, they had never seen Catherine so angry before. She was one of the few women in a town known for never losing her cool. No one had ever thought they would get to see the day when Catherine blew her stack.

Keeping true to her reputation, Catherine was a patient woman. She could handle stressful situations with a calm demeanor and incredible grace. But it's like the saying goes, beware the fury of a patient man. In this case, it was a woman, furious for her only son's safety.

"Miguel," she exclaimed, as all the two dozen voices died down flat. The crockery on the tables, the glasses, even the wall hangings trembled. Miguel halted and turned around to

face her very slowly. *"You damn well know that Patrick is the only person I hold precious in my life!"* Miguel gulped as the wrathful mother raged on. *"I am very disappointed that the thought of sending Patrick to the Caribbean even crossed your calculative mind when you know very well Blackbeard is out there!"*

Catherine knew everybody was watching her, but it didn't unsettle her. *"If anything happens to my son, I will personally come after your head. You mark my words!"* she pointed her fingers straight at Miguel, stared with her eyes wide, turned around, and dashed out of the pub.

Once she was outside, the anger evoked a flood of emotions in her as she burst into tears.

The next morning, Patrick got up at dawn with a mixture of excitement and eagerness. He was anxious to board The Black Marlin and set sail on the adventure that awaited him. He whistled a tune as he got dressed. He could smell the aroma of freshly cooked eggs, which meant that Catherine was already up. Not showing any signs of unease, Catherine filled her son's belly and blessed him on a safe trip while hugging him goodbye. Patrick sensed his mother's fear, but this was definitely the most important day of his life as a captain. Catherine watched him ride off with her heart stuck in her throat, praying, *"May God protect you, my son."* Minutes later, he arrived at the port in high spirits.

Miguel had gotten to the docks early to speak with Patrick. After seeing him arrive, he trudged over to Patrick, who instantly was struck with the presentiment that something was about to go very wrong. Miguel cleared his throat and tried to avoid Patrick's gaze as he said, *"Patrick, I think there's no need to go to the Caribbean in pursuit of my ship. It will be very hectic for you. Why don't you just continue with the usual route, the one oft traveled and used by other merchants as well? It will be easier and also a lot safer for you if you think about it ..."*

Miguel tried every possible excuse with which he could try to convince Patrick to change his mind. He even put himself down, saying that he had been reckless earlier when he appointed the task to him out of impulse. But there was no chance in the world that Patrick was going to let go of that once-in-a-lifetime chance to cross the Atlantic Ocean. He listened to all of Miguel's precautions and concerns, and calmly refused, urging Miguel to stick by his word. His boss was caught in a tough position because of what Catherine had said, but he could not go back on his word. Not knowing what else to do, Miguel assented and allowed Patrick to have his way. He hoped for the best, for if anything went wrong, Catherine would have his head on a pike.

Patrick wasn't out of the woods just yet. His crew was quite skeptical about the trip as well. They had heard about Blackbeard and questioned their captain's sanity for taking a route that would put them in a jeopardizing path. Patrick caught the scent of their agitation, so he assembled his crew members and spoke to them. He addressed their fears and inspired confidence in them. He motivated them to the best of his abilities.

He said, *"Even if the rumors are true and Blackbeard exists, we have one of the fastest ships in the ocean. Blackbeard wouldn't be able to catch us if we all work together. If you think that we do not have it in us to take this ship to its maximum speed, then I will stay in Gibraltar, and we can go back and board our cargo ship."*

The crew looked at each other, confused for a moment, but they took their time to ponder a bit. After a few minutes of reflection, a sailor from Patrick's crew walked towards the Black Marlin, stopped, turn around, and shouted, *"ay laddies, this ship won't sail itself to the Caribbean." "Unless you mate have anything better you'd like to do, what do you say we all get together and plunder Blackbeard's ship?"* The crew started laughing in sequence at this wild allegation, but one laugh encouraged another until they were all having a good hearty laugh. They stood up, saluted their captain in turns, then dispersed and started loading the ship. Patrick smiled wide. He, as well as his crew, knew that they were one of the best seafarers in Gibraltar to sail the Atlantic Ocean, and now it was their time to prove it to the rest of the world. No one could stop them now, not even Blackbeard.

The ship was soon ready to depart. With goodbyes said, they hoisted the anchors and cruised for an adventure which none of them would ever forget.

Back in Gibraltar, while Patrick was away on his voyage across the Atlantic, Miguel had decided to work on Patrick's trade route with a different crew. Not only did he need the distraction, but he also had to take the time to inform his clients about new trade items that would be available soon.

A few days into Patrick's trade route, Miguel entered the port of Tangier. Little did he know of the pleasant secret he would learn about that very morning. Once the ship was tied down and secured, Miguel descended the ramp onto the dock. He stretched, then made the sign of the cross, a ritual he had adopted and performed at every port. While doing so, he noticed two young ladies walking towards his ship. As they got closer to the ship, Miguel recognized Ahmed's daughter, Sabah, and waved. Sabah waved back and smiled. She seemed incredibly happy to see someone she knew come off the ship. Although perplexed by their presence, Miguel waited until they got closer. They seemed to be there for a reason, and he was the only ship docked at the port. Sabah reached Miguel and greeted him. *"Good morning Mr. Captain Miguel. Is Captain Patrick working with you today?"*

Miguel startled but charmed, *"Well, good morning to you, Sabah, but although I like a lady that knows what she wants, will you not introduce this charming lady to me before I answer your question?"*

Sabah replied, *"Yes, captain, sir! So sorry ... this is my cousin Fatima and her and Patrick are in love and will be wed very soon!"* Fatima blushed while Miguel chuckled, neither of them expected to hear anything remotely close to what came out of Sabah's mouth.

"Well now, excuse me manners, lady Fatima." Miguel bowed and took her hand. *"It is an absolute honor to meet a Captain's bride so early in the morning. Top of the morning to you my dear."* Fatima blushed, even more, this time, but got interrupted by Sabah's indiscreet clearing of the throat, *"Uh-huh, Patrick is with you, yes?"*

Miguel took a step back and answered, *"Unfortunately he is not with me today, he is sailing to the Caribbean as we speak. It is a new trading route being established, which I will be announcing today at the marketplace."* Fatima was taken aback. *"Excuse me, Captain Miguel, but when do you expect Captain Patrick to be back?"*

Miguel replied, *"Oh Lord, he left just a few days ago. I would not expect him back before a full lunar cycle. But he will be unloading here in Tangier before sailing back to Gibraltar, it's more convenient that way."* Both ladies were startled by Miguel's reply. Again, fate had cheated Fatima from allowing her time with Patrick. She hadn't seen him since his illness, though she had heard that he had made a complete recovery. The absence of communication was extensive, and Fatima was stretched out thin. She knew men weren't the ones to worry much, but she was hoping for a little sign, a little something she could hold onto until they met again. Despite that, fate was still at a disadvantage for Fatima. The girls thanked Miguel and walked back to the marketplace.

Sabah walked into the store first, followed by Fatima, and upon entering, Sabah saw Ahmed behind the counter. She asked, *"Papa, where is the Caribbean?"*

Ahmed smiled at Sabah and said, *"Ah! Do you remember the story I shared with you last week about the pirate called Blackbeard?"* Sabah nodded with intrigue, *"That is where this pirate is doing some very bad things but there's nothing for us to worry about, the Caribbean is far south, on the other side of the Atlantic Ocean, we're safe here."* Ahmed confirmed.

The girls looked at each other with an anxious look on their faces. Ahmed caught the impression on their faces and said, *"Ladies, it's okay. As I said, it's safe here. There is nothing to worry about. By the way, how is Patrick doing, you did meet him at the docks this morning, yes?"*

They both replied with a fear gripped in their voice, *"No, Miguel told us he's sailing for the Caribbean."* Ahmed dropped the knife he was holding and lifted his foot to avoid getting hurt. *"What??? No!"* He walked out from behind the counter and stepped outside, saying, *"Okay, ladies, let's go have a little chat with Miguel ... "* Ahmed pulled up his horse and buggy, ordering the girls to jump in. Within seconds they were headed back to the docks to see Miguel ...

A week later, in the Atlantic Ocean, the Black Marlin and its crew were soaring in the ocean. Fortunately for them, the weather was fantastic, and it had been a smooth ride up until that point. Of course, while having one of the fastest ships on the ocean, they had to attempt getting her up to top speed. Patrick even insisted on it. It was good practice for his men. No one really knew if they were going to need it or not, but they might as well be prepared.

The ship responded well, Patrick and his crew were able to get the Black Marlin up close to 25 knots. Talking about Knots, at that speed, he was having the time of his life up in the crow's nest. In Knots' world, there were blue skies and a lot of blue ocean but no sight of land. It felt like living a fairy-tale. As they got closer to the Caribbean, that scenery of all blues did change momentarily. Knots couldn't make out what he was looking at because it was simply too far, but it was definitely floating in the water. Knots rang the bell to alarm the captain. As soon as Patrick looked up at him, Knots pointing towards the starboard side of the ship. Patrick pulled out his spyglass, but they were a little too far to make out what was in the water.

"Right standard rudder, steady as she goes," Patrick ordered the helmsman. Everyone was curious to see what was in the water. As they got closer to the debris, Patrick took out his spyglass again to get a good glance. What he saw was not very promising. The wreckage appeared to be from Miguel's first ship. The Maiden of the Sea had been torn to pieces, he could tell from the insignia painted on a piece of plank floating in the water. He instantly bellowed to his crew to get back on course.

"There isn't much to see, men," Patrick lied to them, folding the device back into his pocket. *"Helmsman, hard rudder left, steady on course,"* Patrick ordered.

The ship was approaching the Caribbean Sea earlier than they had expected, and since there were no survivors from the ravaged ship, there was no need to stop for a little debris. They were proud of their progress and thus reverted to their course without asking their captain questions.

Patrick had his doubts and started thinking that maybe Blackbeard was not a myth after all. But he wasn't about to share his suspicions with anyone onboard. Panic, paranoia, and chaos on a ship could be much more disastrous than any pirate, and he knew that much well. So, with the sense of protecting the honor and confidence of his crewmen, he entered the Caribbean Sea without telling a soul about Miguel's sunken ship.

The following day, their destination was in view – The Settlement, where the sun hung warmer and skies stretched bluer. The tropical air surrounding the place made everyone on the Black Marlin ooze with awe. It was certainly a sight that no one on board had ever seen.

Chapter 21
Black is Back

The Black Marlin was directed to a slip as it entered the port of The Settlement. Although the weather, as for the view, was quite outstanding, a lot of people possessed a somewhat sinister air. This was quite awkward being in a British settlement. Everyone but a few actually looked like pirates.

Without wasting any time, Patrick ordered his crew to unload the cargo. But before they got busy, he gave them clear instructions, *"No one is allowed to leave the port for any reason at all."* The crew looked at him and then at each other. Patrick repeated himself and called out to the crew, *"We will be leaving for Tangier as soon as all the trading goods are loaded on the ship."*

Patrick's announcement surprised the crew, particularly because he usually allowed them a good night's rest before leaving the docks. But since the Caribbean was a different journey and a very long one away from home, they had no objections to leaving earlier than later.

Patrick stepped off the ship to greet a dark-skinned, bearded shipper at the dock. He welcomed Patrick with a nod of the head. Patrick indulged, *"Excuse me, sir, would you be kind enough to point me in the direction of Mr. Stede Bonnet, I was told that he is very popular here at the Settlement and I would have no problems finding him."*

While ignoring the question altogether, the shipper confirmed and couldn't take his eyes off the ship. *"Iy... A resurrection me lord, I could have sworn your ship to the bottom of the Caribbean (spit). Black lives to tell the tale, be certain of that he-he!"*

Whatever little hope Patrick was holding onto, plunged after hearing that. He snickered and managed to keep his composure, maintaining with a hint of pride, *"Scratch ye spyglass ol' fella, ya looking at thee Black Marlin. She's thee fastest lady in the sea. Even if Blackbeard were on me tail, he would need a multitude of sails just to catch up to me ship, so there's nothing to worry about."*

The shipper took a good look at Patrick, then his ship, and chuckled with a belly laugh saying, *"He does, he does indeed,"* the shipper replied.

In his gut, Patrick felt terrified of Blackbeard. If what the stories said were true, and the notorious pirate had built the reputation of being swift in the ocean, Patrick had all the reason for being alarmed. Although Patrick showed much trust in the Black Marlin's speed, he really had nothing to compare it to.

Patrick asked again, *"Now that we've settled that ... Stede Bonnet, where can I find him?"*

"Sorry Captn', Stede was not expecting you, he's out at sea. He too suspects your ship at the bottom of the Caribbean Sea, but ... he did say that you were welcome to his villa if you did arrive, a week ago. It might be wise to leave in the morning, me think we're in for thee big storm this evening. It'll get real messy out there ... savvy?"

Patrick had a bad feeling about staying on this island, even for just one night. He thanked the shipper for his hospitality but confirmed that they were leaving as soon as the cargo was loaded. Patrick returned to the ship and decided to give a helping hand to his crew. The crew was taken by surprise at his awkward behavior. He justified it, saying, *"The faster we're done here, the faster we'll be on our way."* Patrick had a bad feeling about this port and that sentiment felt to him like it wasn't safe for anyone foreign. Was he paranoid? Maybe, he thought, but he would rather be safe than sorry.

The ship was finally loaded and ready to sail. As they were pulling in the plank to get ready to leave, the shipper came running to the Black Marlin, asking to talk to the captain.

Bewildered, they put the plank back down so Patrick could descend onto the dock and meet with the shipper. When they were vis-à-vis, the shipper advised Patrick again that it would be better for them to leave the next morning because a storm was definitely on the horizon. *"You wouldn't want to be caught in the middle of one of these storms,"* said the shipper with his thick Caribbean accent.

Patrick thought and considered this information quickly; he did not know this man; he felt he couldn't trust him; for all he knew, the shipper could have been one of Blackbeard's ally. Who was to say Blackbeard wouldn't show up in the morning to steal his cargo?

"Thank you for the warning, but we will be on our way, we'll simply sail to avoid it," he affirmed while leaving the

shipper alone on the dock. The shipper stared for a couple of seconds then shrugged.

Patrick got back on the ship and ordered his crew to set sail, and within a few minutes, off they went. Everything looked good up ahead. The tides were high, and the winds were blowing favorably. Reassured, Patrick decided to take a few minutes to rest in his cabin and closed his eyes.

He drifted off to sleep for what could have been a few minutes to an hour, then suddenly, the continuous ringing of a bell shook him out of bed. He donned his hat, ran out of his cabin, and looked up at Knots, pointing to the back of the ship towards the sea. Patrick strode to the upper rear deck of the ship and looked out to see that a ship was right behind them. What he saw elicited only one thought in his mind: *Blackbeard*.

He pulled out his spyglass to take a closer look at the ship. Searching for something in particular, it took him a moment or so but Patrick did find it. Upon seeing what he was looking for, his heart skipped. There it was, the black flag of piracy with the skull on it at high mast.

Frantic, he turned around and yelled to his crew, *"Deploy all sails and fast, we need speed… Move it, move it, move it!* Patrick's crew all knew what this meant, but having practiced the drill, they were ready for any eventuality. *C'mon men faster, faster… We need this NOW!"* Patrick affirmed.

He gritted his teeth and glared back at the pirates, feeling the immensity of responsibility on his shoulders. He had a whole crew under him who could well be in the jaws of death.

He turned around and joined his crew. It was now time to see how fast The Black Marlin could sail. The shipmen heaved, and the sails were adjusted to feed on the greater force of the wind. Once it was up at full velocity, they seemed to be launching off, leaving the pirate ship behind. The boost was bigger than any speed the crew had experienced, but they weren't relishing the thrill just yet for the pirate ship's sails had not yet been adjusted for acceleration.

The next sight stunned the men on the Black Marlin. The pirate ship deployed a web of hundred sails that made them accelerate even more rapidly than the Black Marlin.

Patrick desperately tried to keep his crew together but panic reigned onboard. They were easy prey for the pirate ship that was gaining on them faster than they could've imagined. They were right not to celebrate too early. Patrick still decided to cling on to hope, and almost on cue, the winds began to blow stronger, giving them a chance to escape.

Minutes passed, and it finally seemed like they were going faster than the pirate ship, leaving them behind for good. The crew started cheering with joy and burst into applause with cheers. They were sure that a miracle had transpired because the pirate ship had let go of their trail. Patrick still had a nervous smile on his face. He was not going to feel joyous until he was back home.

Suddenly, Knots started ringing his bell like a madman. A look of dismay was found on all the men's faces as they couldn't have imagined the pirates catching up to them so swiftly. Their line of sight was directed to the back of the ship and there was currently a lot of distance between Blackbeard's ship and the Black Marlin, simply because Blackbeard had stopped the chase. Patrick's men looked up at Knots again and realized that he was pointing to the front of the ship. Everyone looked ahead to see what Knots was so frantic about, and it was a terrible sight, one that was much worse than Blackbeard and his band of pirates. They were looking at a massive wall of smoke and mist headed towards them like an ungodly wrath. It was a storm, one, unlike anything they had ever seen before. This was undoubtedly the reason why Blackbeard stopped chasing the Black Marlin. At the speed they were going, the crew had no time to turn around and change their course. If the storm caught up to them and struck the ship while it was sideways, it would devour it to splinters. Patrick's mind went numb at that moment; he didn't know what to do.

The panic of his men shook him from the daze. Patrick had to think quickly because although the storm wasn't widespread in the ocean, it was speeding right towards them, and they had no time to sail around it. Most of Patrick's crew were staring right at him and asking him for his command. He thought hard about this conundrum.

The waves coming towards them were at least twice the height of the ship, if not more. The only way to save the ship and his crew was to confront the storm directly, head-on. There was no other way and not a lot of time left to react. The action had to be taken now for them to have any chance of survival. Patrick breathed deeply and ordered the crew to gather as much speed as they could. They all thought he was crazy, raging on a suicide mission, but they got to work immediately. Deploying every sail available to them, the crew thrust the ship into full acceleration. Knots swung from one mast to another against the vicious winds. He was the only one quick enough to tie down and secure the sails to the mast. The winds were ferocious, which worked in their favor; going faster didn't prove to be as difficult a task as they had assumed.

The ship was rolling on the ocean like a bowling ball while the storm approached like a dart. Instead of cowering, the men decided to stare death right in the eyes as it grew enormous. There was no way their ship could resist the impact of the storm heading their way, nor could it slide out of the storm's path, ruining the relatively secure perpendicular angle. The ship looked like a drop of water in the ocean against a tsunami as it ran into the storm at full speed. Frightened to death, Knots came running down from the crow's nest and jumped into a wooden barrel situated on the main deck. Once inside, he picked up the wooden lid next to the barrel, crouched, and closed the lid tight.

From within the barrel, he could easily breathe from a small hole. He had seen enough madness from the crow's nest for a day and this way he felt much safer.

Patrick screamed out loud, dripping with sweat, *"All men below deck! Hurry, all men below deck!"* Mayhem broke out as panic took over their senses. They began squirming and tugging at each other to get to the deck below. Despite the hassle, everybody got in on time. Patrick, who was at the helm with a rope, made a prayer while waiting until the very last minute to steer the ship exactly where he wanted it to go.

The storm was rumbling and seething above him, a furious amalgam of water and wind, seemingly reaching up to the skies like a giant. Once it was extremely close, Patrick tied the ship's helm and ran to his quarters. The rest of the crew below deck prayed while they braced themselves for impact as the storm finally collided with full force.

The whole ship had been trembling long before the impact, so one could only imagine what calamity the storm would subject it to. However, the ship had accumulated enough speed and it sailed upwards along the wave's circumference to reach the crest. As the ship climbed, everyone aboard the ship backed up into a wall. The members who didn't have anything to hang on to ended up falling and tumbling until they hit an obstacle that could be clung to. As the ship climbed, gravity and inertia acted and decreased the ship's speed.

Just as it was about to sail over the crest, the wave broke, and the front bowsprit of the ship plunged into the wave. There was a deafening sound of cracking wood as the ship abruptly slowed down while piercing its way into the top of the wave. The crew was thrown forward, crashing and tumbling as the ship almost came to a halt.

Patrick catapulted headfirst into his mahogany dresser and passed out. The bowsprit had broken off with the force of the wave's impact, and the sails were flapping around in the counter winds of the storm due to the lack of movement. Everything was enveloped in the roaring force of the ocean and waves, loud enough to pierce eardrums and powerful enough to gobble up a town.

In no time, the flapping of the sails loosened the knots which were secured to the masts. And as the wave broke, it launched a massive amount of water down onto the ship while breaking the main mass at its base. All that was unfastened on deck disappeared into the ocean like little balls of cotton. Patrick's cabin was flooded in the blink of an eye. The captain regained consciousness as soon as the cold water splashed at him. The mad influx of water rendered him helpless and near to admitting defeat. The ship by then had crossed over the crest and was riding along the backside of the wave. Patrick and his crew had no idea what was going on outside the ship. In their minds, everything was in utter chaos. They knew that their little adventure was far from being over.

The ship sustained an incredible amount of damage; the hull was deluged with water, the bowsprit was dangling, masts were broken, and few sails were punctured. This meant that another wave, even half as big as the first one, would surely sink the ship. The ship was now on its descent, drifting towards the trough of the wave.

From a listless halt, it was looking ahead ready to catch a maddening speed. Patrick, who was sprawled atop a cabinet, and his crew, scattered around below deck, felt the drift's g-force. They were frightened, their eyes glazed over with hopelessness, convinced that they were at their end. The ship was free-falling down the slide of a wave, and against all odds were they to survive the upcoming crash? Blind sighted, that's what the crew thought. Nevertheless, that's when a life-like miracle happened. Because of the speed at which the ship was racing down, the loosened sails detached themselves from the boom. This was inevitable due to the force of the wind in the sails and the weakened knots. Although the front bowsprit of the ship was broken, it was still attached to the ship. The ropes from the bowsprit were linked to the masts, which created a tremendous amount of pressure on the masts to lean forward.

At the speed the ship was traveling, and because the main mast was cracked at its base, the impact received gave Patrick and his crew a chance to survive. The ship sailed downwards to the trough of the wave and met a huge impact that broke every mast on the ship.

As the ship slid down to the base of the wave, the masts came falling forward, and the sails came down following the masts, all fell onto the ship. Had there been any man underneath them, he would have battered. The ship didn't come to a complete stop after sailing to the trough of the wave and had enough speed to grind up and down along the water surface and that was the end of the monstrous wave. But the ship was off course and was about to be hit by another big wave. It was not as big as the first one, but still huge enough to sink it. While Patrick was trying not to drown in his cabin, he was momentarily disrupted by a bright light streaming from outside the ship. This was the effect of the sails covering the ship, but Patrick really didn't know what that brightness signified. At that moment, it had a dazzling and divine beauty about it.

The ship was out of control and heading for another big wave at a 45-degree angle. Only seconds before the wave slapped the ship to destruction, a counter wave fared towards it and practically neutered it. The front of the ship, however, had turned and was now facing the wave head-on. The ship finally got hit by the second wave, but the fallen sails covering the entire ship provided a cover to the vessel, making it somewhat waterproof. All the water deflected off the ship, and the Black Marlin made its way through.

This wave had supplied the ship with enough speed to sail out of the storm. The storm that soared behind the crew lasted a few more minutes as the ship continued to sail in the ocean. And then, everything became calm. It was unexpected and miraculous how things panned out in their favor, but no one had found it in themselves to speak just yet.

The storm might have been over, but their trauma was not. After tens of minutes, the crew finally dared to move from their spots and emerged from their hiding places, while being grateful for seeing the light and being afloat. Patrick opened his cabin door and cautiously walked outside to find himself under the sails of his ship. He was certain the Black Marlin had suffered a lot of damage, but since the sails covered the entire ship, there was no way of knowing just how much damage was done.

The worse part was obvious; they did not have a mast to tie the sails anymore. The crew started coming up from the hull and gathered out on the deck. They were pleased to see their captain, but Patrick kept a distance because some of them were soiled from top to bottom. Once everyone was on deck, Patrick ordered a headcount. He was grateful to find that everybody on the ship looked accounted for. This had to be a miracle. There was no other explanation for any of it.

But, although miraculous, they were soon to notice someone was missing on the ship. It was Knots, the only one on deck who hadn't responded to his name. One of the crew members explained that the sails were not tied down properly. So, once the extreme winds untied the sails, they followed their masts and fell onto the deck, covering up the ship and keeping it from filling up with water. That was probably what saved everyone's life.

Everyone knew that Knots had been scolded on more than one occasion for his carelessness when it came to tying up the sails. But on this day, they were grateful for his negligence. Patrick shouted out with a chuckle, *"Okay, Knots, you can show yourself now. No one is going to scold you today!"* Some more voices rose in support of the captain, cheering the little man.

Everyone waited, but there was no sign of Knots. Patrick didn't like the feeling that was growing inside him. Something wasn't right.

One of the men stepped out of the crowd and said, *"Captain, I saw Knots, and he won't be answering your call. I saw him jump into a wooden cheese barrel, and I remember seeing him put the lid back on once he got in."*

That's when the crew noticed the stark, empty deck. Things that hadn't been tied down got washed away with the storm, as they naturally should have. With that evidence, there was but one conclusion to be made. The barrel that

Knots was inside had washed away along with the other barrels. The clouds suddenly felt darker. Everybody fell silent, feeling a twisted sadness in their stomachs. They were alive because of Knots, the little man who did not have enough strength to secure the sails. Because of him, the ship didn't fill up with water and sink to the ocean's bottom. But he, himself, hadn't made it.

Patrick took off his soggy hat, closed his eyes, and cited a little prayer for Knots. He did not let himself or his crew mourn for too long since they had more pressing matters on their hands. He swallowed the growing lump in his throat and ordered his crew to repair the mainmast as quickly as possible. Patrick explained, *"We now know with certainty that Blackbeard is not a myth, and as long as the mainmast is not fixed, we are easy prey to this infamous pirate. But I can assure you that when we get back home to Gibraltar, we will have a proper funeral for our little lad."*

The crew got the message, loud and clear. They understood that the mainmast had to go up as soon as possible to resume sailing. The pirate ship was nowhere to be seen, but they had run severely off course and had no clue where they were. The only mission now was to get their affairs back in order to keep the ship moving and pray that Blackbeard did not decide to show up again. Meanwhile, in the Atlantic Ocean, not very far from the Caribbean Sea, a British Naval Ship was patrolling in search of Blackbeard mostly, but any kind of piracy was against the law regardless of who the captain was on the ship. The British Navy came across debris in the ocean and decided to collect it and bring it on board.

This debris came from the Maiden of the Sea that was sent to the Caribbean by Miguel. Much to their surprise, the cargo they snagged out of the water was supposed to be delivered to Tangier in Morocco. The Brits were a little concerned with this situation because they hadn't received any information that Moroccans were dealing with or sailing in the Caribbean Sea.

Finding this to be unusual, they decided to open an investigation and deliver the merchandise themselves to have a clearer understanding of what was going on. After a few hours passed, right before sunset, the Black Marlin's crew managed to secure the mainmast. Patrick's ship was ready to sail. Having just one mast was not ideal for speed but enough to get them home, which was their only goal.

Who knows, maybe on their way home the crew might even have time to repair another mast and get there faster. Patrick could feel his crew still filled with grief and sorrow at losing Knots during the storm, but they couldn't focus on that right now. Patrick was empathetic to their feelings, but there was not much he could do. His own sadness was burdening his heart, especially since he was the closest to Knots. He understood that, at this moment, it might be a good idea to take point and give his crew a little bit of encouragement. So, he spoke to them as a friend rather than the captain of the ship.

"Friends ... gather round, I'd like to speak to all before we set sail," Patrick waited for his men to assemble on deck and began speaking as he looked out to his entire crew, *"Knots ... wasn't just a crewman. He was one of our own. He was a friend, a companion that we all had the good fortune of having with us during our many travels. He was the most caring and generous soul I knew ... He saved us all today, and we should value our lives now more than ever because we stand here because of him. He passed away as a hero and he will always be remembered, in our hearts, and our prayers."*

The crew chanted, *"Hear, hear,"* in unison. Their lives, the breaths they took, and all the life lived after today, was a gift handed over by Knots. The men were extremely grateful and resumed their duties after the tribute. Within a few minutes, Patrick and his men were ready to set a course. Patrick had examined the sea maps and determined exactly where their ship was situated. They had drifted north in the Caribbean Sea but not very far from the Atlantic Ocean.

Patrick gave them the directions with his spirits high and laughed as he told his men, *"All sails ahead laddies! Let's see how fast she can get us to Tangier. We have to catch up with destiny."*

While everyone grinned and chuckled, Patrick felt a warmth in his heart after mentioning Tangier. This warmth could only come from one place, Fatima. After seeing Brian die in his arms and now losing Knots to a storm at sea, Patrick looked up at the skies and convincingly said to himself, *"Okay, this is quite sufficient! If you want something badly enough, you just have to go out there and get it ..."* Determined now more than ever, and to whatever means necessary, he was soon going to meet with the woman he loved. This was his destiny ... or was it?

Chapter 22
Destiny

A few weeks later, a ship entered the port of Tangier. People were informed of its arrival, and the news spread fast around the marketplace. Everyone thought it was Patrick's ship entering the port, but when some gathered to welcome him back, they found out that it wasn't Patrick's ship, but a British naval vessel.

Many of them were confused to see a British naval ship in the port. As the ship anchored to the dock, a British commander stepped out, observing the surroundings while also looking for someone who could explain the debris found in the Caribbean Sea. Ahmed walked in front of the crowd and told the commander that he was possibly the best person to talk to.

Sabah also wanted to follow her father on board. The commander, having quickly judged their relationship, did not have any objections. He allowed Sabah to get on board with her father.

The commander took a moment to tell everyone that they posed no danger to the people of Tangier; they were simply there to try and solve a matter at hand. He then invited Ahmed onboard. *"I am just looking for an explanation or a piece of information that you might share with me that could help me determine if a pirate in the Caribbean, did indeed plunder and sink a ship that might be known to you,"* said the commander. The commander brought them both to the area where the debris was stored, thinking that they might recognize something.

Fatima had recently returned to Tangier with her cousin Hanane. Of course, this was in view of making sure she was in attendance for Patrick's arrival. She was currently present in the crowd and feeling the presence of a British naval ship in Tangier wasn't exactly the best of news. She was worried sick about Patrick, who happened to be behind schedule. Hanane also made the trip to Tangier and like Fatima, she could also tell that something was wrong.

The commander showed the debris to Ahmed. He then showed him some remnants of the cargo that was supposed to be delivered to Tangier. He asked Ahmed if he knew who was supposed to deliver it.

"Here is some debris that was taken out of the Caribbean Sea close to the Atlantic Ocean. Most of the labels we found identified your port. Do you know what ship was transporting these goods?" asked the commander. Ahmed suddenly felt an awful apprehension in his stomach. Without answering the commander's question, Ahmed asked him if there were any survivors from this tragedy.

The commander had sadness in his eyes. *"There were no survivors,"* he said. *"We looked around for a while, but our search was fruitless, and we found no one around the wreckage."*

Ahmed felt like all the wind was knocked out of him. Sabah, who had been rummaging through the debris, pulled out a piece with Miguel's emblem. She showed it to Ahmed before running off the ship, as fast as she could. She did not want to be the one to announce the tragedy. Brian had been enough of an emotional torment for her; she had no desire to live another one.

Ahmed stood up with the broken piece of a wooden crate in his hands, looking at the emblem and informed the commander. "We know this ship, and it is owned by a gentleman named Miguel in Gibraltar. He owns business docks near the port, you'll find him there. Just look for his emblem." Ahmed handed the wooden piece to the commander. The commander took the emblem, gave it to a crewman, and nodded his head, which illustrated that information was shared. The commander then looked at Ahmed and said, *"Sir, I would like to offer you my condolences. Evidently, you and your daughter knew people on this ship, and this seemed to have caused your daughter a lot of sorrow."*

Ahmed replied, *"You are correct, but just not some people, we knew everyone who sailed on this ship. Especially the captain ... and his reputation at sea would have you suspect that his ship was most definitely plundered."*

As Ahmed approached the plank to exit the ship, he lifted his head and saw Sabah run away rapidly from the crowd. Ahmed then scouted the crowd and found Fatima right where he had left her and Hanane before walking onto the ship. This was not going to be easy, but Fatima needed to be informed of the tragedy. He was before her when his eyes started to water. The aged man opened his arms to her to indicate the bad news. Fatima looked up at her uncle's face with glistening eyes and took a step back. Her chest felt hollow and knees weak. She dropped to the ground and shrieked with soul-crushing anguish that made all the perched macaws and crows scatter away. She hit Ahmed as he tried to pull her into a hug while she was struggling with pain. The fears she had tried to dismiss as mere thought for days had just become real. She was not ready to bear the grief thrown at her.

The commander was caught in a situation that he didn't quite understand but quickly put the pieces together thinking that loved ones on that ship were going to be missed. Every onlooker was in shock; they empathized with Fatima's loss. They didn't know what to say or how to console her as she wailed endlessly. Slowly, they walked away from the port and made their way to the marketplace, but before leaving the port, Ahmed had invited everyone to his place.

When they arrived at Ahmed's store, Sabah had prepared light snacks and refreshments for the people who wanted to stay awhile to commiserate on this unfortunate turn of events. She knew her father very well, and not having people over would have been quite unusual and improbable. As people were walking into the store, Sabah came face to face with Fatima. As she glimpsed at her cousin's state, the emotional memories of losing Brian came rushing back. Sabah then embraced her cousin with a hug, saying, *"There's no bigger pain, but you'll get over this pain, just like I did. It feels much worse today than it will tomorrow. One day at a time will get you where you need to be."*

Fatima hugged her cousin a bit tighter as a gesture of understanding and created a distance between both and excused herself afterward. She needed to be by herself, this unfortunate news was a lot to process. Fatima explained that she didn't know a lot of people from the marketplace and didn't really feel like socializing. Even though most of them knew Patrick very well, which made matters increasingly heart-breaking for Fatima. Ahmed didn't think it was a good idea to leave her alone, but nothing he could say would make a difference. So, Ahmed respected her wish and let her have her way as she made her way to the small kitchen in the back room.

Fatima pulled out a chair from the table in the middle of the room and sat down. Feeling so much agony and despair, she crossed her arms on the table to cushion her head upon them and let her mind drift away. She had suddenly become a shell of a human being, and her life had no meaning whatsoever. Patrick had become her everything, despite having shared scarce moments with him. It was the power of fantasies that had exhilarated her soul. But now, she wondered whether her life had any meaning at all. Her love for oneself had fallen into the abyss of doubt.

One person had become the source of her joy, hope, and happiness. This man had become the air she breathed, and the love so natural and intertwined that had been taken away from her left her feeling despondent. All the hope there was for her future evaporated from her world, and she could not see, in any way imaginable, how she could achieve this happiness again.

While trying to submerge her thoughts into good memories of the past, Fatima decided to visit the one place where she found comfort and solace when she thought of her loved one. Yes, indeed, the cliff. She stood up and walked to the doorway slowly, looking out to make sure no one saw her. Then she left using the backdoor, which led to the mountainside behind the port.

As Fatima rambled towards the cliff, her whole body felt numb. All she could think about were the brief moments and memories she had shared with Patrick. The first dance they had together, his courage and tenacity while hiding in a carriage floor just to meet with her, his quarters on the ship, their first kiss …

As she got closer to the peak, close to the cliff, she was convinced that she would never be able to get over the grief of losing him, the pain was too great. The only way for her to be reunited with her love was to defeat life with death. She decisively entertained that thought. Only then would she be able to join him in eternal love.

Out of devastation, nearing the top of the cliff with the sea and the port beneath her, she had taken a firm decision. She breathed in slowly and let her veil loosen then float away in the wind. She yearned to be as free as the fluttering piece of fabric. The idea was too liberating, and there was no turning back from it.

As Fatima was making her way to the cliff, Ahmed decided to check up on his niece to make sure she was fine. When he entered the small kitchen, there was no one to be seen, Fatima was not there. Ahmed thought that maybe she had locked herself in the water closet. Girls have a habit of doing this when they are sad and do not want to give grounds to their sadness, he thought. But this was always all for nothing because swollen eyes gave it away every time. Ahmed walked behind the chair where Fatima was sitting, into a little hallway, then to the water closet's door. He knocked and called his niece's name, "Fatima?" There was no answer. He turned the doorknob slowly and entered the room to find no one there, "Hmmm." Puzzled, he wondered if she could have walked past him while he was talking to other people.

Making his way back to the front of the store, he noticed the back door was not secured, which was doubtlessly uncommon. Although bizarre, for the time being, he thought nothing of it and secured it, then continued his way to the front of the store. Finding Fatima had become a more pressing matter for him at this moment in time.

Ahmed entered the front of the store and started asking people about Fatima's whereabouts, thinking that someone may have seen her, but many people just shook their heads, saying they haven't seen her.

Ahmed was very annoyed, not knowing where his niece was, and as a dark premonition of a girl with a broken heart invaded his thoughts, he spoke loudly to everyone in the room. "Please … Please, has anyone seen my niece,

Fatima?" The room went quiet for a moment while people reflected on the question, some for a second time, but still, they had the same answer. No one had seen Fatima since she made her way to the kitchenette. Hanane was helping Sabah with refreshments when Ahmed frantically posed his question to everyone. She felt that it was important to tell him that Fatima liked to go up to the cliff to comfort herself and enjoy her solitude. Ahmed remembered the back door not being secured and asked Hanane in a pleading voice, *"Sweetie, can you run-up to the cliff to make certain she is not there?"*

Ahmed's tone of voice gave away the emotion as he begged Hanane to go to the cliff. Immediately after, everyone in the room became genuinely concerned about Fatima. Hanane removed her apron, gave it to Sabah, and dashed out of the house towards the cliff to have a look, hoping she would not find Fatima there. As she reached halfway up the mountainside, she saw Fatima standing on the cliff's ledge. That's when she had an awful thought as she watched her cousin looking out at sea. Hanane turned around and saw everyone in the store gathered outside at the bottom of the hill, waiting for her response once she caught sight of

Fatima. Hanane shouted to them, but she was too far up the mountain, and no one could hear her clearly, so she ran down until they could hear her.

"Fatima is standing on the ledge of the cliff, HURRY ... PLEASE HURRY ... PLEASE!" And she let herself fall sitting, to the ground, out of exhaustion, panicked and out of breath.

In a flash, people were hurrying up the mountain, hoping to reach Fatima in time. Most of them walked anxiously up the hill, screaming her name, hoping that she might answer.

Fatima stood on the ledge, extremely focused on her thoughts; she couldn't hear a thing in her surroundings. She had closed herself off to the world as if in a state of hypnosis, planning to reunite herself with the love of her life.

Everyone was so engaged with Fatima standing on the edge of the cliff that they didn't notice Patrick's ship had just entered the bay.

In the broken ship, from a distance, Patrick caught sight of something very odd and disturbing on the cliff. He could see people running up the side of the hill, and he could actually see someone standing on the edge of the cliff.

"Bloody hell, is someone trying to kill himself," Patrick stated as if it was none of his concern. Being extremely curious, he quickly pulled out his spyglass to take a better look. What he saw in the next few seconds chilled him to the bone. He removed his spyglass, looked at the person on the ledge, and then looked again through his spyglass. He could neither believe nor understand what he was looking at while a chill crept up to the back of his neck.

It was Fatima, standing on the edge of the cliff. Patrick, alarmed and confused, had a bad feeling about what he just saw. He had to do something and fast. In a hysterical state, Patrick instructed his men to ring the bell quickly. The ship wasn't even close to the dock, so his men did not understand what Patrick meant by that.

Patrick, utterly panic-stricken, turned around and yelled, *"I want someone up there to ring the damn bell, NOW! And don't stop ringing it until I tell you too ... Anyone, go ...!"*

Without Knots, the task was a bit more challenging for the crew. Patrick turned back to his spyglass, and he saw the girl he loved more than anything in the world, inching her way towards ending her life. This was entirely senseless, why was she doing what he thought she was about to do.

Under his breath, he prayed, *"Oh dear, don't jump, please save her, Lord. Don't jump, Fatima. God, please find a way to hold her back, don't let her jump."*

Fatima's grief had transported her to another realm, and she had closed her eyes as soon as she got to the edge. She stood there, breathing slowly, in and out. In a state of deep meditation to feel a scent, even a small presence of Patrick's heart coming from somewhere in the sea. Slowly, Fatima started to lean forward to take the plunge. She brought her arms out toward the sea, palms facing the sky as if she were reaching out to someone, asking them to take her away.

She leaned forward a little more, almost to the point of no return. But suddenly, her stream of thoughts was interrupted when she heard the stringent piercing sound of a bell ringing frantically. In her confusion, she recognized the sound; the sound of a ship entering the port. Could it be Patrick? Or was this a sign – a sign to let go and make her way back to her loved one? She wondered if her mind was playing tricks on her.

A strong urge to look out to see who was ringing this bell came upon her. Fatima stopped leaning forward, opened her eyes wide, and looked ahead. As her vision cleared, she was able to sense the shape of a ship that got bigger as it sailed towards her. Squinting, Fatima also glimpsed at a man waving his hands and shouting out her name. At this moment, all her senses came alive, and they all spelled out one name, Patrick!

Fatima, unaware of her surroundings, lowered her arms as she tried to move forward to get a better look. In doing so, her foot had landed on a loose rock, and her heart rose to her throat as she tripped and fell sideways, parallel to the ledge.

Within seconds, her body was on the ground, held upward by her elbow, which lessened the fall's impact into the grass. When she opened her eyes, she could see the ocean water right beneath her. Her left leg hung from the cliff while the rest of her body was hinged to the surface. She was safe; she hadn't fallen off.

Fatima didn't even feel the pain of the bruises she had gotten from the fall, but she did burst out into tears of ecstasy and grief altogether once she realized Patrick was alive. She pleaded forgiveness for the act that would have taken her life. Patrick witnessed Fatima's fall as his heart literary stopped beating until she hit the ground. Holding tight to the ramp of his ship, his head bowed, and he thanked the Lord for having him arrive on time. Others saw Fatima fall to the ground as they were coming up the hill, but they froze at the thought of her plunging to certain death.

The closest one screamed out, *"She's okay, she didn't fall off ... She's fine!"*

They couldn't thank the Lord enough for his mercy ...

All they could do was watch in amazement as she sat up crying. They were relieved and thanked the Lord for sparing her life. Everyone heard the sound of the bell. Those who knew Patrick recognized him on the ship's bow – it was him, her savior.

Ahmed was simply thrilled to see Patrick entering the port and started jumping all over the place, shouting his name while waving at him. He couldn't believe his eyes. It was really Patrick. He was still alive.

Hanane was one of the first people to reach Fatima. She helped her get up from the ground, wiping little rocks and sand off her dress. Fatima's emotions were all over the place, but they had switched from life-threatening thoughts to those of love. She tightly hugged Hanane, saying, *"He's alive! Oh God, he's alive, Hanane!"*

Hanane could feel Fatima's heart pound with excitement against her chest. She replied, *"Yes, yes, Fatima, he is! Now let's get away from the edge of the cliff before something terrible happens."* Hanane cautioned while leading the way. Fatima followed as they slowly walked down to join the others.

Patrick's ship was getting closer to the docks, but Patrick was so anxious to get to shore that he took off his boots and dove into the water, then swam to the closest dock.

Although his intent was to see Fatima as quickly as possible, the Brits had a different plan for him. Patrick was arrested and escorted to the British Navy ship for questioning as soon as he got out of the water.

The commander of the British Navy was still at the port and saw this event unwind in its entirety from his ship, but he had noticed a lot of damage to Patrick's ship as well as seeing Miguel's crest on the side of the ship. Since the commander judged that the men on this damaged ship might have some interesting information for him, he felt it necessary to have a little discussion with its captain. Everyone was a little weary of seeing Patrick being taken to the British Navy's ship because they weren't sure the commander would let him go. An hour went by, and finally, Patrick was free. The commander had all the information he needed and would be heading back to the Caribbean. The commander was quite pleased to talk to the young captain about his first journey to the Caribbean Sea. He felt better equipped for his mission to capture Blackbeard, especially after Patrick shared the information he had about "The Settlement." Patrick walked onto the dock and was cheered by his crew. The people from the marketplace were also there to welcome him back.

Although everyone celebrated Patrick's return, most were a little confused by the recent turn of events. It was said that even the British commander could not understand what was going on when he saw Patrick's ship.

No one ever knew that Miguel had two identical ships that could cross the Atlantic Ocean. The first one to leave for the Caribbean had been sunk by Blackbeard's pirate ship and recovered by the British Navy. However, even if there was a second identical ship, which no one knew about, it still could have been Patrick's ship that was sunk. The people of Tangier were so amazed to see Patrick and his crew alive that he felt obliged to tell them his story. The fact that Patrick was alive and well took away the spotlight from the incident with Fatima. Although Patrick was recounting his travels, he did it out of respect for their culture. Amazing as the story could seem to everyone, he really was focused on looking for Fatima in the crowd that surrounded him. He couldn't see her anywhere though he longed to know if she was alright.

Ahmed, being very close to Patrick, knew exactly what he was looking for and interrupted his story, *"I am sure you'll have lots of time to narrate about your adventures at sea, but I do have to tell you that there is someone that has been longing to see you for a very ... very long time."*

Ahmed turned around towards the dock, and the crowd opened up, creating a passage so Fatima could finally greet her loved one. The moment Fatima had a clear route in front of her, she ran towards Patrick with every atom in her enlivened self. She jumped into his arms, and he lifted her off the ground with a hug. They embraced each other for the longest time without a care in the world, merging their lips for a kiss without being wed. From that day on, they were never to be separated again. They would travel the seas together and experience infinite adventures. Two lives that were meant to be had finally met their destiny. After all their separations and sufferings, they were ready to enjoy a blissful life together. Oh ... by the way, you should know that a week or so after the storm, another British Navy ship was scouting the Caribbean Sea for pirate ships. But instead, they found a little man floating in a wooden barrel. Indeed, it was Knots. Although Knots was able to live off cheese and rainwater for a week or so, he had grown a bit too weak to travel, but he was to be returned home soon, to "his" ship in Gibraltar, just how he explained it to the Navy Commander!

THE END

PATRICK KIMMELL